The Use of Dreams in
Couple Counseling

Marie-Louise von Franz, Honorary Patron

**Studies in Jungian Psychology
by Jungian Analysts**

Daryl Sharp, General Editor

The Use of Dreams in Couple Counseling

A Jungian Perspective

Renée Nell

Translated by Sandra Jellinghaus
Edited by Daryl Sharp

Library and Archives Canada Cataloguing in Publication

Nell, Renée, 1910-1994.
The use of dreams in couple counseling: a Jungian
Perspective / Renée Nell; translated by Sandra Jellinghaus;
Edited by Daryl Sharp.

(Studies in Jungian psychology by Jungian analysts; 113)

Translation of: *Traumdeutung in der Ehepaar-Therapie.*

Includes bibliographical references and index.

ISBN 1-894574-14-1

1. Dream interpretation. 2. Marital psychotherapy.
I. Sharp, Daryl, 1936-. II. Jellinghaus, Sandra.
III. Title. IV. Series.

BF175.5.D74N4413 2005   616.89'1562   C2005-902225-6

INNER CITY BOOKS
Box 1271, Station Q, Toronto, ON M4T 2P4, Canada

Telephone (416) 927-0355 / Fax (416) 924-1814

Web site: www.innercitybooks.net / E-mail: admin@innercitybooks.net

Honorary Patron: Marie-Louise von Franz.
Publisher and General Editor: Daryl Sharp.
Senior Editor: Victoria B. Cowan.

INNER CITY BOOKS was founded in 1980 to promote the
understanding and practical application of the work of C.G. Jung.

Cover: *Balance 1/1,* relief print, by Vicki Cowan.

Printed and bound in Canada by University of Toronto Press Incorporated

Contents

Introduction 7

1 Basic Concepts of C.G. Jung's Analytical Psychology and His Theory of Dreams 9

2 The Dream as a Key to the Psychological Situation and to Psychological Types 27

3 The Use of Dreams for Diagnosis and Prognosis 41

4 The Dream as a Barometer for the Counselor 55

5 The Role of Dreams in Group Therapy 65

6 Dreams as a Guide in the Final Stage of Counseling 83

7 The Case of Mark and Debbie 114

8 Summary 126

An Interview with Renée Nell 148

Bibliography 152

Index 153

See final pages for descriptions of other Inner City Books

Though we seem to be sleeping
There is an inner wakefulness
That directs the dream,
And that will eventually startle us back
To the truth of who we are.

—Rumi.

Introduction

Psychotherapists of many different schools use dreams in individual therapy, but few use them in couple counseling. Often, marriage and family therapists have no experience in this area because dream interpretation is not included in their training.

Before I realized the great value of dream interpretation in couple counseling for both the couple and the therapist, I approached the problem from the behavioral side. I used unconscious expressions like slips of the tongue, inappropriate laughter, movement of the hands and body language in interpretation. From time to time I also considered a dream, a drawing or a poem.

Nevertheless, after a short time I had the unpleasant feeling that I didn't know to whom I was talking or what we were really talking about. I was unsure because I had too little contact with the unconscious of the partners. In the sessions I often empathized most with the one who spoke last.

For example, during the first visit of a biochemist and his wife, the man said to me, "I'm sure you will understand that now and then I have to work at night—I enjoy that. But I would like to work without fear that my wife will make a scene when I come home."

Of course I understood that. I made my professional pokerface and said, "Hmm," in a colorless way. Then it was the wife's turn.

"I would like to see how you would react," she said, "if you waited and held dinner from seven o'clock until nine with no phone call—nothing! I missed my evening exercise class. All week long I look forward to that class, but I couldn't go because I couldn't leave the children alone. By 11:00 I still hadn't heard a word. Finally I went to bed. But that's not all. At one o'clock in the morning he came home and was singing happily and loudly in the kitchen while he made himself something to eat. Then he came into the bedroom as if it were ten in the morning and told me all about his experiment. I just hit the ceiling! And now he reproaches me for not being interested in his life's work!"

"Of course," I said to myself, "she's completely right! That is impossible behavior." I was caught in the same unproductive conflict as the couple. Thus I decided to work with couples in the same way that I had worked for years with individuals, namely with their dreams. As soon as I did so, I felt that I was on firm ground. Then other therapists asked me to familiarize them with the use of dream interpretation when working with couples. This led to a seminar, and soon after, a publisher asked me to write a book about it.

For me, the decisive reasons for using dreams in couple counseling are the following:

1. From the very first meeting, dreams show connections between the observed behavior and the underlying unconscious dynamics.

2. Dreams shed light on conflicts that lead to tension and projection.

3. Dreams confront each partner with his or her basic character traits and the deeply rooted causes of their problems including sexual difficulties.

4. Dreams allow insight into the transference situation, which facilitates discussion of relationships in general and sexual problems.

Beyond that, I use dreams for three stages in marriage counseling, whether or not it is therapy of a long or a short duration.

In the first stage, I use dreams for the diagnosis of the psychological health of the two partners as well as for a tentative prognosis. In the second and longest stage, dreams show the reaction of the unconscious to the therapy, and also give a clear depiction of the transference situation. In the final stage dreams can indicate the future development of the couple's relationship. In this stage dreams often indicate the appropriateness of ending the therapy.

Dreams spontaneously elucidate central relationship problems right from the beginning, thus supporting effective and efficient use of the counseling process.

1
Basic Concepts of C.G. Jung's Analytical Psychology and His Theory of Dreams

Jung sees individuation as the highest goal in life. By individuation he means the full development of all our individual attributes. Of course no one can ever reach this state, but we can have as our life-long goal to come as far as we can to full individual development. Jung's philosophy and school of analytical psychology support this process.

The meaning of each therapy, and of each marital counseling, is to help the human being enter into a dialog with oneself as a way of embarking on the process of individuation. The person who responsibly enters into this work will experience individuation as a goal, and will continue to work in this direction.

One of the main tasks in the individuation process is the reconciliation of opposites in our psyches, especially the opposition between the conscious and the unconscious mind. Dreams create a bridge between these two worlds. Jung sees the dream as the ongoing endeavor of the unconscious to create equilibrium in a person, by showing what would be necessary to achieve balance. Our conscious thinking represses knowledge of our inner dualities or our inner opposing desires. In order to reach a balance, the unconscious makes demands on the dreamer that he or she does not want to accept.

A young priest who had recently completed his studies at the seminary and felt tremendously important in his new vestments had the following dream:

> I was celebrating a solemn mass in the largest cathedral in the city; the church was filled. I was sitting on a golden throne. Suddenly great laughter erupted from the congregation. I became very unsure of myself, looked behind me, and realized that I wasn't sitting on a throne at all but on the toilet.

9

The dream shows the dreamer that he is an ordinary human being with normal human needs. The understanding of this message could help to free the young man from his inflated self-importance.

On the other hand, a completely different message was sent to a woman who had a natural gift for writing, which she couldn't accept. She dreamed:

> I was in a dark forest and was led forward as if by magic. I followed a supernatural, beautiful, silvery light that was shimmering through the thicket. As I finally came to the illuminated place, I found a large silver penholder tied to a tree. It emitted a supernatural beautiful light. My initials showed clearly on the penholder.

She awoke, startled that such a beautiful gift should belong to her.

Such good advice and deep truth are not always so obvious as in the above examples. Jung developed a system of dream interpretation that can serve as guidance for the therapist. He thought it was necessary to interpret the dream on both the objective and subjective levels. For example, a young man dreams:

> I saw Aunt Margaret coming toward me on the street, but I acted as if I hadn't seen her and crossed over to the other side.

On the objective level, the dreamer viewed Aunt Margaret as a cantankerous member of the family. He did not like her at all, and avoided her whenever possible. One should explore, however, what kind of street it was in which they met in the dream. It turned out that the man had had a business appointment with a woman on that street the previous morning. He said that the woman reminded him of the aunt in many ways. She was also very aggressive. He was glad when the appointment was over, but he had no idea then why he so disliked the woman. The dream clarifies this now.

On the subjective level, things looked completely different. The following questions are asked: What personality traits do you share with Aunt Margaret? In what way are you aggressive and cantankerous? What do you do to avoid meeting this attribute in yourself? In the dream you look away and cross over to the other side of the street. Do you also look away from your own contentiousness? The next question on the subjective level is this: What provoked your own contentiousness at the meeting yesterday with the businesswoman?

It is doubtless more important for the dreamer to deal with his own aggression, especially since he would like to avoid that problem, than for him merely to learn that the woman reminded him of an unpleasant aunt. Of course both interpretations have to complement each other. In this case the aggressive manner of the woman provoked his own aggression, which he had to repress in order to achieve a positive result in the meeting.

The interpretation on the subjective level has the advantage that the dreamer learns about his unconscious dark side. Jung called this unconscious part of the personality the shadow. This confrontation with his shadow does not come from the therapist, who does not know the dreamer. It is the dreamer's own unconscious that gives him the necessary information. He learns further that the dream neither disparages nor criticizes him. It doesn't even confront him. The dream will only show him how he can change something in himself. It is important that the dreamer learns from the beginning that he is not responsible for what he dreams, but that he is fully responsible for what he does with the acquired awareness.

Regardless of whether one interprets the dream on the objective or subjective level, it is important to take the dream literally. Thus, in this dream cantankerousness means cantankerousness. The aunt in this case is only a symbol for this characteristic and does not stand in addition for a mother figure or a symbol of sexual aggression, etc. It is sometimes very difficult for the beginner to follow this simple rule: *Take the dream literally!* The temptation of the beginning therapist is to project one's own interpretations and associations onto the dream. Taking the dream literally helps to avoid this.

Jung differentiated between two levels of the unconscious, the personal and the collective. The personal unconscious is born with us and dies with us. It contains the contents that we accumulate during our life and is therefore contemporary. In the previous dream the contents belong to the personal unconscious: the aunt, the street, the dreamer's avoidance of the aunt, as well as the associated characteristic of contentiousness.

The collective unconscious contains information and images that can be described as part of being human. Although we have no scientific proof concerning the inheritance of images from one generation to another, nevertheless we do have much empirical evidence, especially in the animal kingdom. There we call it instinctive knowledge. For example, the salmon returns upstream to the place of its birth to lay its eggs. Then it tries to get downstream again, though it usually dies in the attempt. The young salmon know without instruction when and where they have to go and when the time comes to return to their birthplace. What we call instincts in animals are inherited predispositions. These let most animals know who their friends or foes are, what food is good or bad, how and when to build nests, to mate, and much else.

In the unconscious of humankind we find universal archaic images of the same sort. However, they are not as concerned with getting food and surviving as they are with the participation in the experiences of generations of people. They have left behind impressions that perhaps have more to do with psychological rather than physiological survival. We find expressions of this inheritance in myths, fables and fairy tales. We are all familiar with the idea of God in myths and in images as well as the notion of heroes, witches and giants. Angels and devils, the Wise Old Man and the Wise Old Woman are only a few of the many images from human history that populate our collective unconscious. Jung called these enduring symbols the archetypes of the collective unconscious.

Archetypal dreams are signposts for months, sometimes years, to come. They have their own language with something of a lofty, even sublime nature and are distinguished from the everyday language of the dreamer. The dream of a young woman at a turning point of her life can serve as an example. The twenty-six-year-old married woman had tried for years to bear a child. She had had several miscarriages. Finally she was able to give birth, but the child was crippled and very sick. At the time of the dream the child was about to die. The mother was completely shattered and didn't see how she could ever again return to a normal life. At that point she had the following dream:

> I was in a square field surrounded by woods. I wanted to lie down on the ground, but was afraid that some kind of harm would befall me. Suddenly I was sitting at a weaving loom belonging to an old Native American man. All of the threads were tangled up and the more I tried to untangle them, the worse it became.
>
> I started crying. The old man appeared and came up to me. I told him that I couldn't even learn weaving by myself. Everything went wrong. He put his hand on my shoulder and said, "I'm going to be your teacher." I looked up at him and said that everything in me was so tied up in knots that I doubted whether I could ever learn to weave.
>
> He said, "The knots will loosen when you can accept the gentleness, the care, and the love that I am giving to you."
>
> I understood what he meant: peace would come with his help. "How do I learn to weave?" I asked.
>
> "Learn to accept the emptiness inside yourself, to feel it, and to wait. That is the way to learn weaving." He smiled at me and said, "This is a beautiful day to lie down in the field in the warm sun and go to sleep."
>
> I wasn't afraid of the woods anymore.

The archetypes that are particularly important in connection with couple counseling are *anima and animus*.[1] Anima (Latin for psyche) is for Jung the symbol of the soul, of the feminine as a function. It is the principle of the earth, of feeling. The anima incorporates wisdom and those creative forces that are symbolized by conception, pregnancy, and the birth of a child. The anima is eros, the chthonic power underlying life. For the man the anima is the contrasexual part of his

---

[1] As already mentioned, the collective unconscious is populated by many other archetypes, but they don't have an important part within the framework of this book. When they appear here in a couple's dreams they will be explained in connection with the counseling.

personality. Every male is born with an anima function. Men have more or less of an anima quality, just as they are endowed by nature with more or less intelligence or artistic talent. As with other qualities with which we are born, the development of the anima can be either furthered or hindered through one's education and the socializing process. The truth of this is shown clearly in dreams.

The anima in a man's dreams is always symbolized by a feminine person. She might appear as a happy little girl, an old hag or a dying child. She could be a crippled woman or from a different social level. She could come as an unattainable, incredibly beautiful fairy-tale princess. In every case the dream shows how the man relates to his own feminine side and therefore also to females in his outer life. A man who dreams of his anima as sick or impoverished experiences his feelings generally as negative. He will try to solve every problem in life through thinking and practical activity. In relationship with such a man, the woman often suffers from his coldness. The task of the therapy is to help him in the unfolding of his underdeveloped feeling side. It is important for the woman to understand that his reserve is not a sign of not caring for her, but of a weak anima.

How far a man is able to go in accepting his anima depends upon the society in which he lives. In a period in which figures such as Goethe's Werther are seen as exemplary, when men write romantic poetry about women and love, when women are looked up to and men talk freely about beauty bringing tears to their eyes—in such a period a man will usually have a different attitude to his feeling side than in a militaristic period. During a Romantic period the feeling, artistic anima-man is considered normal and the one with a lack of feeling is viewed as neurotic.

In a military epoch, the situation is exactly the reverse. Exhausting physical exercise and endless drills serve to train the body for military service. The cadets band together as brothers-in-arms and experience a strong loyalty to their corps. During bellicose times feelings are repressed and even physical pain is not admitted. The youth has to learn to keep a "stiff upper lip" and not to cry. Only women keep journals and write poetry. In such "hard times" women are considered to be a necessary evil, good only for bearing a male heir, running the household and serving their lord and master. However, for a certain type of man, a complete suppression of his anima contradicts his nature. If the environment forces him to repress his anima over a long period of time, neurotic symptoms inevitably develop. Genuine feeling will be repressed and sentimentality will emerge instead.

The reverse is true for the animus, the masculine function in the psyche of the woman. The animus is to be understood as the quality of logic, of thinking. Just as a child of the woman is her own child, so the child of the animus is a visible achievement: a book, a practical accomplishment, an idea. The animus appears as a masculine figure in a hundred guises: as a small child, sick or healthy; as a handsome youth, brutal delinquent, wise old man, or a crippled, senile old man. From the symbols one can tell whether the woman's animus is healthy or sick, mature or immature.

Anima and animus are socially conditioned. At various times in history, women were looked upon as higher beings, having only the purest feelings. A relationship to the world of objects, to objective thinking, was not desired. The animus was therefore superfluous ballast and was projected onto the man. This often led to a neurotic dependence on men. In such a period it was considered unfeminine for women to engage in professional work or travel alone.

The present period has not only liberated the anima of the man, but has emphasized even more the liberation of the woman's animus. For more than a hundred years, women have fought for the right to live their animus qualities in education and in work. They want to have the right to realize their thinking abilities in the object world just like men, without having to identify with the animus completely and without denying their feeling function.

Anima and animus are described here in such detail because they play an enormous role in couple counseling. Jung once said jokingly, "There are always four people present at every wedding: the man and his anima and the woman and her animus. If the anima and animus understand each other, the marriage will go well even if the man and woman fight."

The dreams related in this book will clarify the degree to which the anima-animus problem is the reason for conflict and how understanding this problem relieves the situation and facilitates therapy. Often the question is asked whether a man has an animus and a woman an anima. The object-related ability of man, his gift for creating an outer reality, his activities, are manifestations of a man's animus function. The woman's faculty is to relate to earthy reality, to feeling, intuition, to children. That is her own anima quality. When, in each person, the two sides are in harmony, the man and woman will be in harmony with each other. The task of therapy is to facilitate the best possible balance of anima and animus, in both men and women.

Before we turn to examples, it is necessary to deal with Jung's concepts of the *persona,* the *shadow,* the *ego* and the *Self.* These are decisive aspects of the personality, present to a greater or lesser degree in everyone. Their personifications often appear in dreams.

The persona

Persona originally stood for the kind of mask that Greek actors wore to portray a certain character. Its use in psychology refers to the fact that the persona is not an inborn quality like anima and animus, but is the result of experience. It is the socially accepted behavior learned in childhood, the ability to conform to social norms in dress, language and behavior. A young man who wears torn jeans to a job interview with a conservative firm is lacking in persona. The same would be true if he went to a casual party in a dark suit with shirt and tie.

The persona is most often dreamed as clothing because such images clearly express the degree of one's social adaptation. Adolescence is typically the time for persona problems. The ego of a young person is often still tentative and fears being different from his or her peers. Adolescents often choose to dress differently from adults, to make the point that they are "unconventional." Overlooked of course is the fact that the young person is conforming 100% to the conventions of his or her age group in clothing, hairstyle and speech.

The persona of adults is often expressed in status symbols: the Ph.D., the "right" address, acquaintance with well-known public figures, invitations from wealthy people, etc. If one of the marriage partners is bent on acquiring status, while the other doesn't want to be involved, this can lead to serious problems. The following dream of a married man shows this:

> I'm climbing up a ladder on my house. My wife is supposed to hold the ladder, but suddenly I notice that she is sawing off the lower end. I'm terrified that I'll fall headlong to the ground.

The woman, who also personifies his own anima, is undermining his climb up the career ladder. The dream shows him the danger of trying to climb too high. As he couldn't recognize his own feelings of anxiety in his venture, he repressed them and projected his doubts onto his wife, who did in fact oppose his career path. Thus they often argued.

The persona is the aspect of the personality that is mostly related to the outer social environment in which we live. It is connected least of all with our individuality, but rather seeks to adjust our individuality to society. In starkest contrast to the persona—that is to say our public personality—stands the deeply hidden quality of our shadow.

The shadow

Jung refers to our shadow side as those qualities of our personality of which we are not conscious. In dreams, figures of the same sex may represent aspects of the dreamer's shadow. In a man's dreams, the shadow is a masculine figure; in a woman's dreams, a feminine one. Although the shadow is mostly composed of the qualities in ourselves that we don't like, we see, as in the above-mentioned case of the woman with the gift for writing, that there are people who struggle with accepting their good qualities. They repress talents because they are afraid that they can't do them justice. Often we become aware of our shadow through projection. Qualities that we don't want to acknowledge in ourselves seem to exist in other people. Then we are critical of them for these qualities. For example, if one marriage partner has an aggressive shadow, then he or she will be particularly intolerant of that tendency in the partner without being aware of it.

Even without the help of psychology, people are well acquainted with the kind of behavior that is expressed in quotations like the Biblical one that it is easier to see the splinter in the other's eye than to recognize the mote in one's own. The fact that we are not able to acknowledge our envy, our impatience and our tendency to be self-righteous does not mean that these traits are not obvious to others. For example, gays or lesbians often think that their homosexuality must be hidden. Anyone who has been in group therapy has experienced a situation in which an individual, with great pain, "admits" to being gay, and is amazed to hear from the others: "We've known that for a long time; so what of it?"

Often the opposite occurs. No matter how carefully and gently we try to confront someone with his or her shadow side, it only leads to vehement denial and countercharges. In almost every marriage counseling practice the denial of one partner's faults is just as frequent as their hurtful demonstration.

It is the dream that constantly brings to light that repressed and unconscious material. Most of our dreams aim to bring about a psychological balance. At first, becoming conscious of our repressed qualities leads to doubts and uncertainty. A short dream of a man at the very beginning of his therapy is a good example:

> I was on a dark street. A sinister character was following me. I became frightened and ran up a small street; it was a dead end. The man caught up with me, hit me and threw me to the ground. I was knocked unconscious. My last thought was, "The man is drunk!" When I woke up I was relieved to be in my own bed at home.

I knew only a little bit about this man: that he was a teacher and well respected. I asked him if he perhaps had a secret drinking problem of which he was not conscious. He answered no to my question,

but then became very nervous. I asked him if he had any other de-
pendencies that he couldn't control, much like an alcoholic with a
drinking problem. He nodded silently, his head fell forward, and he
started sobbing. I urged him to tell me his secret instead of tormenting
himself all alone with it. The shadow that pursued him did indeed ter-
rify him. He was a teacher in a girls' school and he was plagued by a
desire to sexually approach pubescent girls. He had never been caught
but lived in a state of fear that he would be. He regarded his current
position in a new school as the dead end that would lead to his down-
fall.

Confrontation with the shadow is often painful, but acceptance and
understanding of it is the first step toward change. Most people do not
confront others with their shadow for fear of hurting their feelings.
People who have been in individual or group therapy are usually grateful when someone, in an accepting manner, makes them aware of
their shadow. Others may react with rationalizations and defense of
their behavior.

The ego

Many psychologists understand the word "me" to refer to my ego;
that is, the total personality. But Jung sees the ego as only a part of
the psychological structure. In dreams the symbol of the ego is oneself, the person I dream as "I." Other people in the dream personify
the shadow, anima or animus, and other parts of the personality, as
we have seen. The "I" or ego is thus only an aspect of the personality
and not a symbol of the total personality.

It is very important in couple counseling to recognize how each
partner dreams his or her own self: anxious, subservient, arrogant,
vain, or as not even present in the dream—which happens often with
people who are very split off from themselves and their own lives.
Again and again people say, "I wasn't in the dream at all." For the
most part these people also have no emotional reaction to what they
experience either in dreams or in daily life. They are passive, often
depressed, onlookers.

There are as many inborn differences in ego strength, or lack thereof, as there are inborn physical differences. The ego often manifests in a dream as the body: "I am sick," or "I have a cold," or "I can't stand up any longer," or "I'm taken to the hospital." Such remarks are often indications of so-called neuroses. Naturally the parental home environment and external events such as war, being orphaned, hunger or illness can contribute to the weakening or strengthening of the ego. However, one should not forget that external events always meet up with an existing constitution, physical and psychological.

Jung sees the ego as the center of consciousness. Its function consists in translating into action impulses from within and without. For example, when the telephone rings, I interrupt whatever I'm doing and answer it; or I remember that my mother has a birthday the next day and go, instead, to the store to buy her a present.

The ego is able to repress impulses that are not pleasant. I "forget" to pay back a loan. I "forget" to tell someone about a call if I don't feel good about the caller.

The ego can be either strong or weak. Instead of ego strength we often speak of will power. Both concepts mean essentially the same thing: energy that is available to the ego. I hear the alarm clock ringing and know that I should get up. The degree of my willpower or ego strength determines my action. Even in a simple illness like a cold, a lot of energy is drawn away from the ego. In such a case I might say, "I usually get right up when the alarm rings but today I simply can't summon the energy." Every neurosis is in fact a waste of will power or, to express it differently, the ego is so weakened by maintaining neurotic behavior that many daily activities can no longer be accomplished or lead to excessive fatigue.

In serious mental illness the disintegration of the ego is clear to everyone. It is usually the first thing the family describes, saying, for instance, "He was always so lively and interested in everything. Now he just sits for hours at a time without moving; even tying his shoes takes forever; he just sits with the laces in his hand and stares straight ahead." We talk about the flooding of the ego by the unconscious. The psychotic might hear the telephone ring but the impulse to answer it is too weak to lead to action. All of the so-called will power is held fast in the unconscious and is not available to the ego. Lay people often reproach someone in this situation, saying: "You're just lazy; if you wanted to, you could get up and go to work." If the person is really not capable of translating impulses into action, due to mental disturbances, such remarks only serve to wound the ego further without bringing about any change in behavior.

It is not always possible to know the cause of a certain behavior. Dreams can be a rich source of assistance here. They can help us identify a deteriorating neurosis in the early stages, before it becomes a psychosis. In mental illness the threatening disintegration of the ego becomes particularly clear in dreams. This is helpful because at times the person can no longer articulate what is going on inside. His family sent a young man to me because they were increasingly worried about his strange behavior. He considered himself to be "completely normal." He told me the following dream:

> I'm sitting in my car and want to drive up the mountain, but the car starts going backward. I completely lose control; it goes faster and faster, and I crash into the side of a house.

A few hours later the family had to hospitalize this man because he really did lose control and went after people with a kitchen knife.

The danger of mental illness or a severe psychological disturbance is often shown in dreams as uncontrollable danger from flood, fire, or, as in the above-mentioned dream, loss of control.

Ego inflation and deflation play an important role in marriage. In the West at the present time, the ego is not understood as just one of several psychological functions. We behave as if we are the owner of all of our inherited faculties and talents, and as if we had created our intelligence. We identify easily with the success of our achievements. We pay the price of identifying with a lack of success in our work with anxiety and guilt. One hears statements such as the following: "I have painted a picture. I won a prize. I am a good painter."

The ego should only ask for recognition of the fact that it was dutiful and steadfast in its work on painting, even when this wasn't easy. Whether or not the painting turns out well or badly depends on many factors: talent, practice and experience, a capable teacher, the necessary time to do the work, and so on. All of that has nothing to do with the ego. However, the ego has the tendency to seize both praise and blame that don't belong to it.

During the Middle Ages there was a different understanding of the ego. Artists often did not sign their paintings; they created them to honor God and acknowledged that God had given them talent. They felt that they had the right to use this talent, but that the praise was due to God. The artist saw him- or herself as an instrument, a servant. Today artists often claim to own creative talent. While such an ego-centric attitude is imparted even to the small child, nevertheless we reproach a person who is conceited or puts on airs.

Deflation of the ego is widely known by the term "inferiority complex." Every ego action is diminished by the word "only." "Oh, I only sketched the picture." "I only won first prize because . . . ," etc. Ego inflation and deflation are closely related. Both come from the tendency of the ego to chase compliments, to take praise and blame upon itself instead of simply seeking satisfaction from work well done.

A further problem is ego weakness. In a marriage this can be interpreted as unwillingness and lead to strife. One hears statements like this, "If you really wanted to, you could certainly do it!" The wish to achieve something can be strong; however, when the ego is weak, the strongest wish avails nothing. We all know the nightmare of lying in the middle of a street or on railroad tracks. The next truck or train will come and run you over. You want to get up, run away, save yourself, but you can't.

The psychologically ill person may be in this situation in real life. To say to such a person, "If you really wanted to, you could do it!" increases anxiety but does not strengthen the ego. The ego quality of each partner in the marriage has far-reaching consequences as to how they relate to life and to each other. Their dreams give us information, thus removing ignorance and misunderstandings.

The Self

Just as the ego, according to Jung's model of the psyche, is the center of consciousness, so the Self is the center of both consciousness and the unconscious; that is to say, the Self is the center of the personality as a whole. The goal of each individual, as well as that of each partner in a relationship, is to shift authority from the ego to the Self.

The values of the Self are essentially of a spiritual nature: harmony, transcendence of the ego, humility. If one lives in the Self, one cannot be hurt. But there is no mortal who can do this over a long period of time. Only saints are fitting symbols of being contained in the Self. Although we cannot dwell for long in the Self, it makes a great difference if someone at least makes an effort toward the realization of the Self or is completely identified with the ego.

The inner psychological relationship between the ego and the Self is revealed in the following dream:

> I want to steal an elegant fur coat in a department store. As I am trying it on, I hear a voice that is so strong it reverberates through my whole being and in all the space outside. The voice says, *"No!"* It is like the voice of God. I begin to tremble, collapse completely, and cry for a long time.

The dreamer had received an offer of marriage that flattered her because the suitor's background was more prosperous than hers. He was a respected man in the eyes of the general public. Unfortunately there were many aspects of his character that she did not like at all. Besides that he was quite a bit older than she and she felt out of place in his circle of friends. Her family pressed her not to reject such a "splendid alliance" and she was tempted by the glamour of the life he offered her. Nevertheless, something in her resisted accepting his proposal. In the middle of this dilemma she had the dream, in which the fur coat symbolized status and wealth.

The position of the ego and the Self becomes clear when one asks: What is it in me that pays the price for my decisions? Do I pay with ethical and eternal values, with the gold of my Self, with the well being of my soul for the transitory gratification of the ego? Or do I make a sacrifice, of my vanity perhaps, or my greed, in order better to serve the Self?

This relationship of the ego to the Self resembles the subordinating of the deeply religious person to the will of God. The ego represents the lesser value and expresses this in words such as, "Thy will be done," praying to understand the wisdom of God's intention and find the strength to go the right way. If one substitutes the word "God" here with the word "Self," one sees what the Self means. The Self is generally represented in dreams by such images as the circle, the ying-yang symbol, the cross, in the person of a wise man or similar spiritual figures.

> I'm walking in the woods. I feel very solemn. I come to a very clear round pond. There are wide stairs leading down. I walk down the stairs and at the bottom of the pond I find a square gold box. I open it; it contains a splendid crystal that emits a heavenly light. I'm overwhelmed, close the cover, and remain sitting very still next to the box. Gradually I fall into a wonderfully deep sleep.

This dream reveals the Self. It is the task of the dreamer to accept the message of the dream and to find the strength to realize it in actuality. Seldom do we see the Self revealed in such beauty as in this dream. More often the conflict between the ego and the Self is presented. The following dream is the result of such an ego-Self conflict. The situation in which it was dreamed was simple. A man was offered a better job. His wife urged him to take it. He was honored by the offer; however, he hesitated without really knowing why. Then he dreamed:

> I'm in Siberia; I don't know how I got there. I have a long whip in my hand and pace off in front of a row of coolies who appear to be poor and

wretched but, nevertheless, stand at attention. An officer walking next to me whispers, "The good thing is that there is a loaded revolver in the handle of the whip; you can shoot the people right away." I wanted to get out of the situation as quickly as possible, but I didn't know how and I was terrified.

The job that had been offered him was that of an inspector. His superior had said, "We really have to take hold. A few heads will roll." Such a job was contrary to the dreamer's nature. He would rather go about his work without attracting attention; however, the money was tempting. The dream warned him that taking such a job would be a betrayal of his Self and would lead to feelings of tremendous anxiety.

The goal of the ego is outer accomplishment and success; the goal of the Self is inner accomplishment and individuation. If the ego can be subordinated to the goal of the Self, then a person feels creative and whole. Almost everyone has had the experience of having relinquished a particular ego wish through inner struggle only to have the wished-for event come to pass without any help from oneself. Then the ego fulfillment has a different meaning, and one can enjoy the reward without having had to sacrifice one's better Self. In the language of yoga this is known as "living from the center."

Understanding dreams

In order to appreciate the interpretation of the dreams presented in this book, one must become familiar with a few basic Jungian principles. The dream is seen by Jung as a gestalt—as a configuration that must be understood as a whole, in the way that a melody, a story or a painting is understood. Therefore one doesn't take this or that part of the dream structure and apply free association.[2]

---

2 [For more guidelines on the interpretation of dreams, see "General Aspects of Dream Psychology," *The Structure and Dynamics of the Psyche*, CW 8, pars. 443ff, and "On the Nature of Dreams," ibid., pars. 530ff. (CW refers throughout to *The Collected Works of C.G. Jung)*; also James A. Hall, *Jungian Dream Interpretation: A Handbook of Theory and Practice.*—Ed.]

The beginning of the dream sets the theme as in a symphony. The middle of the dream develops the theme. The conclusion points out the solution and gives advice as to what the dreamer should do in conscious life in order to put the dream's message into effect. The advice often takes the form of a warning.

The therapist tries to approach the dream in as neutral, nonjudgmental a way as possible and to take the dream literally. One accepts that the dream is often the reaction of the unconscious to the events of the previous day. Also the dream wants to tell us what we must understand in order to bring about an inner balance. Jung refers to this as the homeostatic function of the dream, which is itself an aspect of the self-regulation of the psyche.

When we work with dreams in couple counseling, we ask the partners to write down their dreams and, in addition, to make short notes on the events of the previous day. This is especially interesting because one sees how the same experience is reflected differently by the unconscious of the man and the woman.

In the following chapters the inclusion of dreams and their meaning for couple counseling will be described in examples from various cases.

2
The Dream as a Key to the Psychological Situation and to Psychological Types

The dynamics of the psychological components such as anima and animus, ego, Self, shadow and persona, are different in each individual. Most of us rarely consider these structures. Perhaps one is conscious of being tender hearted or mistrustful of others or very cautious, but we know very little about the connections within our psyches—how one quality influences another.

For example, the so-called generosity of some people may originate from the fact that they are afraid to turn down a request because they don't want anyone to dislike them. Behind this lies the thought, "I don't want anyone to think I'm petty." Throughout there is a fear of being judged by the other, of dependence on the other, and of denial of one's own feelings and wishes.

In couple counseling it is important to search out the inner structure of each partner. Once one has grasped the psychological structure, then the participants may begin to understand each other's reactions in different situations, what is repugnant or appealing, the goals each pursues, and the manner of that pursuit

The investigation of personality usually begins with the couple counselors asking questions and listening attentively to the answers. However, responses can only derive from conscious material. So the couple counselor must read between the lines in order to learn more than the person seeking advice has communicated. Dreams are a great help in this task.

As an example, here is a brief description of a man about himself and the relationship with his wife; then a short dream is related.

Bill, a highly-paid photographer for a magazine, said, "When I return from a trip, I usually have a month off. Then I always build something for our house or for my wife Jenny. The last time it was a painting studio for her. This time she wanted me to build a dark room. I was glad to do the project. But then this!!!!"

He pointed to his broken arm that was in a cast from the shoulder to the wrist.

"For the first time in my life I'm the patient and she really doesn't have it easy with me. I must bore her with my condition. I'm always talking about it—and about all the things I could have done in Africa. That would have been my next assignment. For years I've dreamed of such a chance. Finally the assignment was given to me—and now this!! I'm often afraid that my arm won't be the same—that I won't be able to use the camera. I know that's crazy, but I can't stop talking about it. When Jenny finally has enough and says, 'For heaven's sake, will you just shut up!' I become furious. No wonder she wanted me to see you."

Two things struck me: Each time Bill mentioned his arm and his fear he laughed in a forced and unnatural way; and he took all the blame on himself, emphasizing how good, patient and understanding Jenny was. As sincere as his account was, it didn't tell me much about the man or his marriage or the talented, artistic, understanding wife.

About Bill I knew only that he was gifted, creative, perhaps somewhat too identified with his profession—although perhaps not. He would rather take blame himself than blame another person and was probably someone who would like to live peacefully. All that sounded completely normal. Even the fear of not being able to practice his profession, while not exactly realistic, was nonetheless understandable. Each of us would likely react with frustration in the same situation. What should I advise? How could I help?

I said quite openly to him that up to this point I couldn't see what I could do for him other than wishing him a good recovery. I asked whether he had had a dream since our first telephone conversation to set up the appointment.

"Yes," he said, "It was only a fragment, something completely crazy." I asked him to describe it.

"Jenny ate my arm up," he said. Then he laughed in that forced way again.

Now all of a sudden I knew a lot more than I had earlier. The dream didn't make me clairvoyant, but it led me to ask some crucial questions that took our interview in a new direction.

"He experiences Jenny at present as a devouring anima," I said to myself, "not so good and understanding after all." Perhaps he must assure himself and her that she is constantly good and understanding to appease her because he fears, rightly or wrongly, that she will devour him.

The dream said nothing about whether the real Jenny was devouring and destructive. On the subjective level the Jenny in the dream is his feeling function. Bill's anima was definitely very destructive at present. The questions that now suggested themselves to me were: What is Jenny really like? Does he repress her destructive behavior? Where is his aggression? Not once in the dream did he mention any reaction of his when Jenny ate up his arm. Why didn't he defend himself? That made an impression on me.

I began to understand his psychological structure a little and suspected a certain ego weakness and fear of seeing the negative in himself, in others, and in the world as a whole. Now I could at least pose a few questions.

The first question was routine: "What happened on the day before the dream?"

"Nothing special," he said, "I was nervous, felt useless, couldn't do anything, criticized Jenny who was constantly patient with me. It was a day like many others lately."

"You describe Jenny as a very understanding person, almost a model wife. Why would you have such a negative dream about her? Did you have an argument on the evening before the dream?"

"An argument? No. We never fight. Jenny wishes for something and I fulfill her wishes." Then the hateful laughter erupted again.

"Is that so funny?" I asked.

"I don't know why I said that. I had become angry that evening. Jenny showed me a few photos that she had taken of the house and said, 'It's a shame that I won't be able to have my dark room now. I was so happy about that.' "

"What did you answer?"

"I'm sorry about it too."

"And what did you feel?" He was silent. "I was angry but I didn't think I had any right to be. She hadn't meant anything bad by it."

Then suddenly he began to speak with uninhibited emotion about how Jenny always wanted something—about everything he had built: a doghouse, rabbit hutch, large sun deck, a painting studio. She always wanted something. He had never built anything for himself.

Jenny was not employed. For years she had been finding excuses to do nothing. Now and then she would take some kind of part-time job—she could have taken an examination for teaching art, but she doubted her ability.

"It's not because of the money," he stressed. "I can't find a rational reason for it, but somehow I feel it is really terrible that I wear myself out on trips to distant places while she lies on the sun deck and thinks of the next thing for me to do for her when I return."

In further conversation it became clear that he had never before voiced these thoughts and that he disregarded his feelings with other people too. Naturally that made him very popular, but he hadn't noticed what a high price he paid. Basically he thought that people made great demands on him, which meant he was always busy and had no free time for himself. He was afraid to use his creative skills for himself. He had excuses—his professional work would be routine. His own ideas were no good and wouldn't do justice to his perfectionist demands. For example, he wanted to create a picture book for children. He would much rather have done that than build a studio for painting. Jenny used Bill's flight from his own work for the fulfillment of her wishes and he used Jenny's wishes as excuses to say that what she wanted was more important than the children's book.

So before the first hour was at an end we came to the insight that the broken arm and forced period of rest had confronted him with his anxiety about his creativity and also his fear of inner emptiness.

"Maybe I'm not at all creative," he said, a typical last-ditch effort to justify his behavior. This doubt was the voice of his demanding anima, the symbolic inner Jenny that ate up his creativity, leaving him incapable and empty and then led him to focus on the needs of others. From this standpoint it was almost not important whether Jenny was demanding or not. I realized that, without Jenny, he would probably soon find someone else whose neediness would keep him busy. Suddenly I recalled what he had said about his wife: that she was talented, had a teaching certificate but didn't believe she could teach because she was a perfectionist! Now the Jenny in the dream as anima let it be known how the perfectionist demands ate him up and paralyzed him. At present *that* was the core of the problem. The dream had contributed much to make this clear to me.

In Eileen's case, exactly the opposite came to light. I didn't know Eileen; we met by chance at a professional conference that lasted several days. She was a physician and chief of staff in a hospital, an attractive, "feminine" woman in her mid-forties, with a heart-warming laugh. She came across as a strong person, a woman who coped with life on her own. As an internist she knew little about dream interpretation. She asked if I could explain how I worked using one of her dreams so that she could see for herself what the practical value of dream work was. I asked her to tell me a dream, from the night before if possible.

"Such a short, meaningless dream," she replied. "Even I know what it means—what Freud calls the day's residue."

I said to her that I was not a Freudian, but, as always, I would be glad to hear her dream. She then told it:

> There were a number of crippled men, most in wheelchairs; I was supposed to take them on as patients but didn't want to; the thought was repugnant to me.

I was astonished at this dream—this reputable, hard-working, self-sufficient woman dreaming about crippled men?

She continued: "I will tell you why the dream contains the day's residue. Last night, before I went to bed, I worked on a scientific report about crippled men in our hospital. It concerns veterans wounded in war who have been with us for years. My specialty is working with them. We try to rehabilitate and socialize them. I really like my work; only the written reports bore me and anger me."

I agreed that the dream was a residue of the day, but that I would nonetheless be glad to know what else had happened the day before.

"Nothing," she said.

"There is never 'nothing,' " I said. "You asked me at breakfast this morning, for example, what it costs to send an airmail letter to Brazil. Evidently you don't often write letters to Brazil, otherwise you would have known that. Is there perhaps something special there that you've forgotten at the moment?"

She became very animated. Indeed, she had forgotten that she'd received a letter from Brazil. She had been corresponding for some time with the Department of Health there. She had been offered an incredibly good position with interesting possibilities for research, teaching at the university, and a very high salary. I wondered why she'd forgotten to mention that. I assumed she would be very interested in this offer and that she would naturally accept it. But I had guessed wrong. After hesitating for weeks, she had decided to decline the offer, but had not yet mailed the letter.

Suddenly I saw the whole structure of this personality before me. Her animus side, her masculine function, was crippled. She had said that these men were in the veterans' hospital for seven or eight years, and even longer. I had in mind to ask her what "battle" she had been wounded in about eight years ago. What had crippled her? When had she taken the job in the hospital? Was she stuck there like the crippled soldiers? Had she also lost the courage to leave the security of this position and go out in the wider world? These questions pressed in on me and I almost knew the answers before she gave them.

"Eight years ago—a terribly painful divorce," she said.

A war she had lost. She felt crippled afterward for a long time. "You're still not out of the wheelchair; the dream was yesterday," I said. "Don't you try to bring the veterans to the point of leaving the hospital and getting back into life? How does that pertain to you?"

"From the outside my position looks very good," she answered, "but it is nothing more than a hiding place for me. And yet I can't seem to help myself. It depresses me."

"Who should help—a man?" I asked.

Her eyes filled with tears. "I'm afraid to go alone to a strange country, although I know that this position is a once-in-a-lifetime opportunity. But I don't know if I can meet all the expectations. I don't feel strong enough."

"The dream says that you must care for your crippled animus. But you don't want to; the task is repugnant."

She replied, "I don't even want to know I'm like that! This dream is such a stark confrontation—how can one avoid its implications?"

"You shouldn't avoid them," I answered. "You should listen to the dream, become strong, leave the hospital and accept the position in Brazil."

"That's what you say," she replied. "You don't even know me."

"I don't say it; your dream says it to you in the clearest language—that, after receiving your 'war wounds' from the divorce, you hid away from life."

She answered, "Naturally I know that I should go to Brazil. I'm going to think it over again."

She spoke in the tone of an obedient child who has promised her mother to be better. I told her that she didn't owe me an explanation. I had no intention of acting as her therapist. I had only wanted to show her what help I receive from dreams—that they allow me to see more clearly the psychological structure of a person and to approach his or her problem.

"I understand that now," she said, "and I'm amazed at how subtly the unconscious pointed out my weakness. Most people don't know this side of me at all; they only see my strength, my self-sufficiency."

"That is always the way with dreams," I said. "They always hit the nail on the head in ingeniously creative ways. Our unconscious is usually more intelligent than we ourselves, more creative, and also wittier—that is the reason I'm so eager to work with dreams."

"In retrospect I see the meaning of the dream so clearly," the doctor remarked, "that I wonder why I couldn't see it myself."

"The answer is right at hand," I said. "The dream confronts you, and we all avoid confrontation when possible. The dream demands a decision from you that is difficult and that frightens you. You have strong motivation not to hear the message of the dream."

She nodded. As we were saying good-by she stressed once again that from now on she would not question the value that dream interpretation has in the real world.

Psychological types

In addition to showing the situation in which one finds oneself, the dream also reveals the psychological type of the dreamer.

Jung described eight basic types, each of which behaves in a way that is "typical." The types are built on the four basic functions of feeling, thinking, sensation and intuition. In addition, Jung speaks of two attitudes with which we relate to life: extraversion and introversion.[3]

A comprehensive description of the types would take a chapter in itself. I will confine myself here to the two attitudes: extraversion and introversion. They are called attitude types because they characterize a person's basic attitude to life. Knowledge of the types helps the couple counselor to make extensive predictions about a person's behavior patterns.

During the counseling, each individual learns his or her own type and that of the partner. It is quickly understood how a particular situation may be simple for one type, but difficult for the other, and why the world is understood in such different ways.

It is hard to believe that the terms "extraversion" and "introver-

---

[3] [See "General Description of the Types," *Psychological Types,* CW 6, pars. 556ff. also Daryl Sharp, *Personality Types: Jung's Model of Typology.*—Ed.]

sion" did not exist until Jung coined them fifty years ago. The fact that these expressions are in everyday use in Western culture shows how important it is to comprehend their meaning. Although we all have a vague idea of the meaning of these concepts, nonetheless the following more precise descriptions might be useful. Later we can demonstrate their significance in dreams.

The extravert is attracted to the outside world, to the world of objects and people. Only seldom, and then usually only for short periods, does the extravert turn inward. These individuals tend toward expansion and are very sociable.

The introvert approaches the world in a completely different way. His or her inner nature, the subjective experience, is more important than the outer world. The introvert is not attracted to the outer world; on the contrary, he or she avoids it, seeking not expansion but security and a consistent position. The introvert ventures into the outside world for only a short time, just long enough to place the perceived event or person in his or her inner world.

The difference in types—particularly when the types are very extreme—leads to opposite patterns of behavior and objectives and often to diametrically opposed views of the world. Naturally each of these types develops characteristic neuroses and typical difficulties in life. The extravert flees her- or himself, and seeks the company of other people. Only a breakdown will bring an extreme extravert to a standstill. The introvert, on the other hand, flees the company of others to attain seclusion.

Even apart from these extremes, extraverts and introverts are frequently so different that it is as if they lived on two different planets. In a relationship this difference in attitude can lead to two reactions: attraction or repulsion. Often the attraction of opposites predominates, as when a couple first meets and falls in love. During marital strife the repulsion comes to the fore.

It should be added that each type has the tendency to view his or her own behavior as right and normal and to see the opposite type as wrong or neurotic. For that reason it is important that the partners learn that neither type is better than the other; rather that each type has positive and negative features. Probably the number of good and bad qualities is the same in both types, but the ways in which they are shown is different.

Naturally the question arises—not just for counseling, but also in looking at everyday life—wouldn't it be better for people of the same type to marry? If posed in this way, the question can't be answered. If we think of couples that are similar, we come to the conclusion that they have just as many difficulties as couples that are not. However, their problems are of a different kind.

I am thinking of a husband and wife who were considered to be the ideal pair in their circle of friends because they almost never quarreled. The reason was that they spent every free hour, even weekends, in the club or in the company of other people. Here is a dream of the husband, similar to other dreams he had of this type:

> A cable car was going by faster and faster in front of the same background.

At the same time the wife, who played tennis and spent a lot of time at the club, had the following dream:

> A man at the tennis club was explaining an extraordinary invention to me: a complicated apparatus, an artificial arm and hand that made it possible for each tennis player to play fourhanded tennis. I was very impressed and said that I'd like to buy these extra arms so that every Sunday each foursome could play sixteen-handed tennis.

Actually the two had absolutely no relationship, much less a marriage. Although they were always together, because they didn't share an inner life they had hardly any reason to fight.

This shallow life collapsed like a house of cards when the wife fell in love with a quiet, creative, introverted man who caused her to become more aware of her inner self and to occupy herself with neglected talents.

The relationship between two introverts is frequently as free of tension as the marriage of extraverts, because each person lives deep in him- or herself, unrelated to the partner. In the same sense, this can't be described as a true marriage. It is rather a quiet side-by-side life in which neither person disturbs the other; however, that means that no cross-fertilization takes place either.

There is no such thing as a life with another person that is problem-free, whether one is involved with one's opposite or is joined with one's counterpart.

The decisive lesson as far as types are concerned is to give the partners the possibility of seeing that, for example, the undemonstrative behavior of the other is possibly not based on a lack of love but derives from a difference in type; to see that this type of person expresses affection differently.

Again and again we see that the extraverted person who is always busy still has time to remember the partner's birthday and buy a gift, while the introvert frequently forgets such dates or will work on making a gift but not manage to finish it in time. That is only one of many possibilities of conflict and mutual complaints.

Another question that is often asked is whether it is possible to change one's type. It seems that personality type is inborn. Most mothers remember that their extraverted children were livelier even in the womb than the introverted children who were also quieter and less active after birth. If, through demands from the environment—whether from parents, school or social norms—pressure is placed on a child to change his or her type, negative effects can occur and lead to neurosis. However, there are people who are extraverted as children, become introverted during puberty, only to become extraverts again later in life. Naturally, the opposite also applies. Extroversion and introversion are patterns of behavior that are affected early on in a good therapy. The opposing functions of thinking and feeling, sensation and intuition, are less easily adjusted.

The goal of marriage counseling is not to change the type of one or the other partner, but rather to bring them to some self-awareness. This happens best through clarification of existing differences. The characteristic behavior of an individual is often shown in dreams.

Chuck and Joan, a married couple, are a good example. They were both in their mid-forties and had grown children. Joan didn't work outside the home, but she had many interests and enough money to pursue them. Chuck had a good administrative position with a company. Now and then they had marital difficulties that were incomprehensible to them. They really did want to get along. Chuck admired Joan's varied talents; she respected the fact that he loved to read. While the children were still at home, she had always taken care to see that, in addition to the time he spent with her and the children, he also had enough time for undisturbed reading and for his walks. This quiet time meant a great deal to Chuck.

However, once the last child had left home, Joan wanted to spend more time with Chuck. He felt this as pressure and couldn't explain the effect her demands had on him. Arguments took place and they finally decided to seek counseling. I had advised them, in the time until their first session, to pay attention to their dreams and to write them down, also noting the dates. They did that and brought one dream each that they had had on the same night. On the evening before the dreams, they had been talking about a big social event to which they'd been invited. They both had different feelings and expectations concerning the invitation, and the conversation had once again led to an argument. Both dreams clarify the situation in the finest detail. Chuck's dream:

> I was in a beautiful sunny meadow, full of flowers and grass. I was afraid of the wild animals that could be lying in wait there, so I climbed up a round stone tower. I climbed all the way to the top where I found binoculars with which I could scan the field in order to see if it would be safe to come down.

It is clear, from even a superficial examination of Chuck's dream, that he is the introvert in this marriage. And Joan's dream leads to the conclusion that she is extraverted:

> I'm climbing up a flight of stairs and find a door. I open the door and en-

ter a room filled with people having a party. I feel very satisfied with myself because of my beautiful clothes, which are just right for the occasion.

Without going into detail, it is clear what different feelings both
partners have concerning the upcoming social event. When a room
full of people appears to the husband as a field of wild animals,
whereas the wife is completely comfortable, then it is clear that they
are speaking about different things when discussing the event. It is
also clear why Chuck often isolates himself at parties, which angers
Joan. She, meanwhile, stays in the middle of things, which makes
Chuck envious and angry.

The dreams give the counselor still deeper insight. Chuck appears
not only to be introverted and quiet but at first rather unassertive. Do
the wild animals lying in wait in the field also signify Chuck's own
hidden aggression of which he is afraid? It has already been stressed
that, on the subjective level, every person, animal, or object in the
dream is a symbol for qualities of the dreamer. I considered the possibility of group therapy for him; there he could become acquainted
slowly with his aggression and, with the help of other couples, work
on dealing with it.

A group of married couples helps many people to dare to come
down from the "tower," since in a group one always finds people with
similar problems. Although there was not enough time in the first session to discuss all this, still the dream clarified much about Chuck's
psychological type. This confirmed once again the fact that what was
so simple and enjoyable for extraverted Joan—people, socializing,
brief and superficial contacts—was difficult assignments for introverted Chuck.

Joan's dream also said more than what was already known to her,
that she felt confident and liked social gatherings. Dreams constantly
bring out something unknown, not yet conscious. When a dream appears on the surface to be depicting only the events or thoughts of
the previous day, one must look behind the façade to see whether a bit
of shadow is hiding on the subjective level. This applies also to Joan's

dream, which gives the impression of being rather trivial, but actually has something significant to say. Joan's shadow was her persona problem.

I have mentioned that clothes are often a persona symbol. It is therefore a possible sign of diminished self-confidence that Joan must rely on her dress, her persona, in order to feel accepted. Perhaps it's not only clothes that she needs for self-confidence. For Joan, as a married woman, her husband and children also belong to her persona, including the college her children attended, the title and position of her husband, everything that connotes status in her social world.

Naturally she wanted her husband to shine in company. He behaved awkwardly, however, and was not aware how noticeable it was when he withdrew to page through a book in the library or to go into the garden to look at the flowers. This not only angered Joan but also made her very insecure. Group therapy was as desirable for her as for Chuck, although for different reasons. She needed confrontation with her superficiality as well as support for real self-acceptance. She needed to learn to find her security in herself instead of in the behavior of her husband or in the expensive schools her children attended.

Clearly, dreams can help the counselor to understand the interlocking nature of psychological conflict between people in long-term relationships.

3
The Use of Dreams for Diagnosis and Prognosis

Each individual's level of psychological health is a decisive factor in couple counseling. The degree of the psychological disturbance and also the psychological reserves in each partner helps the counselor plan the sessions.

There are many psychological tests that can give us information. However, I prefer to use dreams in diagnosing the psychological condition of the partners. Dreams answer the questions I pose to myself: "Who are these two people? Am I dealing with neurosis or psychosis? Or is this basically a psychologically healthy couple only needing some clarification and help for a short period?" Depending on what I find in the dreams, I design the kind of treatment that seems most appropriate.

Sometimes it is advisable to take one or both partners into individual therapy for a certain time. Often it is also possible to begin therapy with both right away. Whenever possible my colleague John and I carry out the counseling together. Frequently this kind of cooperation works well because the husband feels supported by the presence of a male therapist. A man who is having problems with his wife may assume at first that a female therapist would be on the wife's side, and this heightens his resistance to the therapy. Sometimes, however, the opposite is the case, for instance when the man feels inferior to other men. He might be embarrassed to talk about these difficulties with another man, and feel more comfortable with an older, somewhat maternal woman like myself. Whatever the case, he hopes that I will accept him like a good mother, with kindness and understanding.

Then again, we have the situation where a couples group offers the best chance of success, especially when the partners feel socially isolated and think they're the only ones with problems. Some people will listen to another member of a group rather than a marriage counselor,

41

because they think: "Maybe *you* can take this kind of attitude (of the spouse), but, after all, I'm not a psychologist . . . ."

However, participation in a group is no guaranty of success. The kind of counseling is not the decisive factor. What makes the difference is that the partners feel that they are in good hands, that they have confidence in the counselors, and, if they are in a group, that the other members understand them.

Three cases follow. I worked by myself without my colleague in the first case. It became evident in the first session that a joint approach would not be possible. The reason for this will become apparent.

Herman and Mary were over fifty years old and had been married for more than twenty-five years. Both their children were also married. Herman did illustrations for books and taught art in high school. Mary ran the household and helped her children, friends and neighbors with cooking and baking. She had recently entered the menopause. Since then she had started to complain not only about the present condition of her marriage, but also about everything that had gone wrong in the last ten years. This was astonishing because up to now these two people had had a quiet and harmonious relationship. Now they argued so often that their oldest daughter, who was a social worker, advised them to seek marriage counseling.

In the first session Mary talked about issues that were completely new to her husband. For example, she complained that he was passive and never helped her with housework. She described him as increasingly slow and impractical. Her anxiety about getting older, something she had never felt before, made her look at his limitations in a very critical light. He barely understood what she was talking about. "But I have always been this way," he said. It sounded like an apology.

In all the years of their marriage, Mary had admired her husband as the artist he was, but now she was increasingly disappointed in his work. His illustrations looked strange to her and they had much less success than before. Every day he went to his studio earlier. However, he now needed a whole week rather than a weekend to come up with a sketch for a new illustration, and even then he didn't produce anything really good. He wasn't really conscious of these facts and had no explanation for them, which only made his wife more frightened.

The husband gave the impression of being a calm, somewhat passive and withdrawn person. He looked older than he was, but didn't seem to be in a bad psychological situation. He accepted the observations of his wife concerning his slowness, but didn't feel that he could do much to change it. He was somewhat anxious himself about producing so little art in the last few years, but he tried to rationalize it.

I asked about his dreams. He said that he dreamed every night, usually terrifying nightmares. His wife confirmed that he often groaned while dreaming and also cried out loudly for help. Whenever she woke him up, he would tell her about the frightening situations that had tormented him in the dreams.

The first dream he told me had occurred just a few nights before:

> I'm going into a deserted factory. I haven't been there for twelve or fourteen years. No one had been in the factory during the last twelve years and everything had slowly fallen apart. No one had come to repair anything. I walk through the factory. It is a bleak sight; all of the machines are on the first floor, just as they used to be. They were good, strong and durable machines that were driven by big wheels from the ground floor. However, all of the transmission belts driving the wheels were cut and the machines could no longer be repaired. Not only were the wheels rusty, they were completely demolished and broken into small pieces by vandals. An auxiliary engine, which had kept the large machines running for some time, was also ruined and no one knew how to repair it. It was a scene of complete destruction.

Associations to the dream revealed that this man had been brutally mistreated by an alcoholic father from earliest childhood. He recalled that he was twelve years old when his father had almost killed him with a butcher knife. The police came just in time to take the wounded boy to the hospital. After that he had failed at school and felt inwardly destroyed. At fourteen he was apprenticed to an uncle who owned a small factory, but he wasn't treated much better there than he had been by his father. He had to hand over to his father the little money he earned by his hard work; his father then spent it on drink. The boy felt deep hatred that he couldn't express. When he was drafted into the army, he was happy for the first time in his life.

After the war he met the woman who later became his wife. She showed a maternal interest in him. She wanted to make him happy, to give him what life had failed to provide. He was hired by a school and was still teaching there at the time of the counseling. In addition he worked as an illustrator for two publishing houses. Life with his wife was simple and quiet. Even when the children came along, nothing much changed for him. He played and drew with the children in his calm way. His wife took care of the house and saw that the children had everything they needed. She made sure that Herman was not burdened with more than he could manage. She never complained. He was a kind person and grateful to her. She accepted her life and was well satisfied with her family.

The auxiliary motor that he mentioned in the dream, and that had kept his own machinery going through the years, was his wife. She had given him a great deal of psychological support, but now that she burdened him with her own fears, he felt that his total existence was endangered. His artistic creativity suffered as a result. This dream and similar dreams that followed left no doubt in my mind that this man was chronically schizophrenic and that the poor little compensation, the auxiliary motor, couldn't help any longer. The prognosis for him was not good. It seemed highly unlikely that he could regain his vitality and creative ability through any kind of therapy.

I therefore suggested that I speak to the wife alone. It turned out that she was a strong, intelligent and very healthy woman. With a heavy heart she accepted the fact that her husband, a man who had been severely damaged from earliest childhood, would not become healthier with advancing age. She admitted that she had suspected this for a long time, but had hoped something could be done. Nevertheless she was prepared to stay in the marriage and to take up the function of "auxiliary motor" again because she really loved her husband, who had many endearing qualities. Her momentary fears over aging were the result of a recent rejection by a man. She had fallen in love with him, but he had preferred a younger woman. This problem was worked out in a relatively short individual therapy.

Another diagnostic dream was much happier than the one just mentioned. A wealthy couple, Fred and Diane, came to see me because they had so many arguments. They had been married for six years. She reproached him for being egotistical. He said that she was driving him to despair with her desire for a career, which he thought would threaten his social position.

John, with whom I shared this consultation, interrupted, "I know that feeling. I was just as old-fashioned at the beginning of my marriage."

Fred replied, "I'm not old-fashioned. Do you think that someone is necessarily old-fashioned if he doesn't want his wife to work?"

"No," answered John. "I only know that I resisted having my wife work because of the old-fashioned ideas of my father."

We didn't want to pursue the argument on this point any further. I'm not quite sure how it came up, but somehow it was mentioned that Diane was in the habit of getting up two or three times a night to see if both her children were well covered up.

"Some women are afraid of thunderstorms," Fred said, smiling. "My Diane is afraid of drafts."

"Yes, it's really ridiculous," Diane said, "but I think that drafts are very harmful. I read once . . ."

We all had to laugh.

"I feel she is really overdoing it," said Fred in a slightly angry tone, "but that's the way she is in everything."

"If you weren't so egotistical," Diane replied, "you would get up and check to see if the children are covered up . . ."

Fred shrugged his shoulders indifferently, apparently used to this reproach.

"I don't understand this whole thing," I said, turning to Diane. "Don't you live in a warm climate where the nights are warm?"

"Not only that," said Fred, before Diane could answer, "we also have a highly paid nanny who sleeps with the children."

"It isn't abnormal that I should want to protect my children from drafts, colds and illness," said Diane, piqued, and it was obvious that we would get nowhere if we stayed on the level of these animosities.

I asked Diane if she remembered a dream. (When she called to make an appointment ten days before, I had told her to try to remember some dreams.)

"Yes," she said, "the night after our phone call I had a dream that I wrote down and brought with me." She read:

> I was with my girlfriend at the movies. After we had left the theater, I said to my friend a while later, "I forgot something in the cloak room of the theater, but I don't know what." The friend said, "You have forgotten your children there. You checked them at the cloakroom before we went into the movie." I laughed and was completely unconcerned. "Oh, the theater is closed by now; I'll pick them up tomorrow."

She added that a few days after that she had had a similar dream:

> I put the children in a compartment of the train and I went in another. When a few cars of the train were uncoupled, I forgot the children, and I never went back to find them.

Both dreams were in strong contrast to her exaggerated solicitude for the children at night. The dreams clarify why she had to show so much concern. Unconsciously she wished to be free of the obligation to the children. Although she consciously reproached her husband for being old-fashioned in not allowing her to work, it soon became clear that she was much more annoyed that the children stood in the way of fulfilling her life's wishes. Still, a direct question like: "Do you feel your children are a burden?" or "Do they hinder the fulfillment of your own plans?" would only cause angry protests. Every therapist avoids that in the first session.

On the subjective level the children represent the young and childish part of Diane herself, the part that she tried to forget. In fact, she had already separated from this part of herself—like the cars on the train. I asked if she liked to play with her children sometimes, or play in other ways—golf, perhaps. She angrily rejected this notion.

"I played enough as a child. My husband, though, can't get enough—he's always playing. Now he's building toy gliders just like a teen-ager. My toy would be a boutique or something like that. That could really excite me."

John very carefully tried to find out to what degree she was conscious of her real attitude toward her children. "For my wife," he said, "the decision between children or a career was not easy. For a long time she felt that the children stood in the way, that they actually robbed her of her own life."

"Yes, I know that feeling," Diane said spontaneously.

Fred interrupted, "And you call me egotistical!" Half apologetically he added, "You have no idea what it's like in my profession. It just won't do if my wife works. It would look as if I didn't earn enough and would result in a loss of respect on the part of my colleagues."

"Really?" I asked in as neutral a manner as I could.

Fred added, "I know it sounds odd, but I can explain it."

John and I said that we were interested in the explanation but it would have to wait until the next session.

After they had left, John and I talked about our diagnosis and the prognosis. We were both quite optimistic. They were capable of expressing themselves. Both were psychologically healthy and willing to grapple with their problems comparatively openly. The two dreams showed, however, bizarre behavior for a mother. That the loss of her children in the dreams caused no guilt feelings seemed strange to John. I agreed, but added that under the circumstances—she wanted so badly to have a boutique and a career—perhaps this unconscious wish to be free of the children ought not be judged too negatively. Besides that I thought she had completely normal guilt feelings.

"She didn't say anything about guilt," said John.

I replied, "I see her nightly visits to the children's room to make sure that nothing has happened to them as an answer to her unconscious guilt and also as a kind of self-punishment."

"Yes," said John, "to pull yourself out of sleep three times a night—that would sure be a punishment for me."

"Somehow she hinted at that when she reproached her husband for being too egotistical to get up, thereby seeming to say, 'I'm not egotistical—I'm making sacrifices for my children.' "

Granted, this was a neurotic way to deal with her wishes and guilt feelings. However, Diane seemed healthy enough for us to offer a good prognosis for the marriage counseling.

Couples almost never come to counseling with the real reason for their difficulties. As we have already seen, the real reason is usually unconscious or repressed, at times manifesting only as a symptom. In the following case, which John and I began together, this misunderstanding was in the foreground.

Nick was thirty-five years old and worked as a printer. His wife Pat was thirty, very intelligent and worked as a teacher. Irvin was their nine-year-old son. They came for family therapy on the advice of Irvin's schoolteacher, who was Pat's friend. They were seeking help for Irvin who had a reading problem.

"He reads so badly that his little sister is already almost better than he," said his mother.

"Is that true?" asked John, turning to the boy.

"That's crazy," said Irvin. "Penny just turned six. She can hardly read at all—besides that, she stutters." He said this with a kind of triumph. He was obviously tired of being made a scapegoat all the time, and rightfully resented that. In this first session it became obvious that the parents believed that all the family problems would be solved it only Irvin would get over his inhibition in reading.

As they left John said, "I would like to work with Irvin alone; I used to tutor children like him when I was a college student. He'll be reading soon, and he'll have fun doing it." I thought that was a good idea.

We both agreed that Irvin probably needed the treatment much less than his parents. We developed all kinds of hypotheses but had no material on which to base them. The situation seemed to suggest that the somewhat cool mother/teacher made too strong demands on her children, thus contributing to the boy's reading problem as well as the stutter of the young girl. We finally decided that careful observation of the three as well as a few dreams would show the way the therapy should go. And that's the way it was.

In the second session the parents brought Penny along and something quite unexpected happened. When she turned on the television set, a children's program came on in which a woman talked very fast to the children, some sort of unintelligible word salad that made the children laugh; however, Penny covered her ears, stamped her feet and broke into tears. She stammered out, "I hate her! I hate her! She's like Aunt Irene. I don't want to stay here!"

Irene was the father's sister, ten years younger than he, who had moved into their home in order to attend college in New York. She helped out with housework and was available to baby-sit in the evening. She was a nice girl but she talked so fast that Penny could hardly understand her. Attempting to talk as quickly as her aunt, Penny had started to stutter, which made her very frustrated. Irvin confirmed that Irene talked fast but added, "She doesn't make me nervous." I was surprised at the word "nervous" from a nine year old. It sounded as if he had picked it up somewhere.

"What or who does make you nervous?" I asked.

He hesitated and appeared slightly embarrassed. John encouraged him to say what was on his mind; no one would think badly of him.

"Daddy . . ." said Irvin softly, "when he always walks back and forth . . . even if he doesn't say anything."

The wife agreed, "Yes, he makes me nervous too."

Gradually one piece after another was added to this mosaic, and we weren't far from the diagnosis. I asked Nick if he had dreamt since our last meeting. He told the following dream:

I was at my parents' house in a small overcrowded room, where three artificial Christmas trees stood. My wife and my sister were sitting down, and I was standing next to the trees. I said that I was very fond of trees, especially oak trees, but added that a harmful kind of beetle was crawling under the bark of the trees. The beetles spread a disease that would kill these trees and all the trees in the vicinity. Besides that, the disease would spread very fast.

In the discussion of this dream it became clear that what was getting "under the skin" of the husband was not the reading problem of his son, but a problem in the marriage. It was his wife who, as the expression goes, got under his skin. Her intelligence and superiority in many areas compromised his position in the household and was felt as a threat to his masculinity. That was the disease. It was almost a repetition of the situation in his parents' house—the much younger sister, who was constantly brought up as being more intelligent than he. Since she had been living with them, Nick had felt pushed aside and ignored by both women. They were better educated than he and had many common intellectual interests in which he did not take part. So he would get angry and pace back and forth without saying a word. He realized that this made his wife nervous, but he hadn't realized that his son also reacted negatively.

Nick's feeling of inferiority made him overly anxious in relation to Irvin. He put strong pressure on the boy to achieve, especially since Nick realized that Penny might possibly surpass her brother some day. He didn't want Irvin to suffer from a younger sister the way he had. Since Irene had moved to their home, Nick had increased his demands on Irvin considerably, and Irvin had reacted with a reading problem. "And Pat doesn't help at all," he said reproachfully.

Irvin added, "At least Mommy leaves me in peace—she says it's not so bad; I'll learn to read later on."

And what do you believe?" asked John. Irvin said thoughtfully, "I think she's right." So it wasn't the cool mother-teacher who put pressure on Irvin, but the father with his feelings of inferiority. He considered his wife's tolerant behavior a weakness.

Now there was still another decisive question. I asked Nick, "Do you ever get on your own nerves? Do you have traits that get under your own skin?"

"Oh, yes—sure." The answer was very spontaneous. "Since my sister has come I feel completely impotent—weak and undermined. But even before, I felt that way toward my wife. I always feel inferior. She reads so much and goes to the theater and museums. Sometimes I go along and even enjoy it—but I'd rather go bowling or play cards with friends. She doesn't like that. She turns up her nose at those things."

John interrupted just as Pat was going to defend herself: "Nick, you were going to say what you don't like about yourself—why you are weak . . .?"

"Yes, I'm always competing with her. I always want to prove something to her—and when I catch myself doing it, I'm angry with myself. Then I say to myself, 'You are really dumb, Nick; they're right, and on top of everything else you're a weakling.' "

His wife looked at him very surprised. She was obviously not aware of what was going on in her husband.

"Have you ever talked about these things together?" I asked.

Both shook their heads.

On the objective level it was his wife who seemed weak to Nick and who got under his skin, but on the subjective level it was the criticism of his own weakness. The fact that this plague—and what a plague it was to have to compete continually with your wife and to continually come out the loser! —could kill strong oak trees pointed out that the vital strength of the man was seriously threatened. The unconscious was sending him a message: You have to end this situation as quickly as possible.

Now we could make a diagnosis. The couple should come to John and me for marriage counseling. John would work alone with Irvin to help him free himself from the pressure to succeed and to develop a healthier attitude toward his younger sister. I, myself, would like to get to know Irene in order to understand why she put herself under such pressure that little Penny was afraid of her fast talking.

I would like to have had a few sessions with Nick alone but that would have been very bad for him psychologically. His self-destructive feelings of inferiority would have led him to say to himself, "Of course I'm the sick one, I need the therapy, my wife is the superior one as always—she doesn't need individual therapy!" I wanted to prevent that.

I was therefore reassured when Pat said to me on leaving, "I'm glad that we can come back again. I would really like to know what I can do to make my husband happier and have a better marriage."

"My wife is always such a good student," said Nick, half admiringly, half sarcastically. "You'll have a harder time with me. I'm not that intelligent."

"You're already competing again," said John, laughing. "There are no good or bad grades given out here; everyone passes."

In order to make the correct diagnosis, it is important to determine whether certain behavior patterns, in a dream or in reality, could be classified as neurotic or psychotic. In Nick's dream about the plague, which could be destructive, a clear warning was given that points to a possible fatal destructiveness. However, in the dream neither the person nor the trees are dead; it's only a warning. The weakness that is symbolized by the plague is of a neurotic kind.

In contrast to that, the dream cited earlier of the desolate ruined factory gives the picture of a completely destroyed person. One would have to describe his psychological condition as severely neurotic. One indication of a psychotic dream is the passive and threatened position of the ego: the wrecked machines in the factory, the auxiliary motor beyond repair. When a healthy ego is not available to put insights into action, therapy can't help much. One would have to try to build up and strengthen the ego in a long drawn-out process. With Nick it appeared to John and I that such an attempt could succeed.

As already mentioned, the body, the "I" in the dream, often symbolizes the ego. Just as it is impossible to do gymnastic exercises with a completely wrecked and weakened body, so it is also senseless to do therapy with a psychologically crippled person. In such cases one should only try to make life a little easier for the patient.

Of course, one always has to take the total situation of the dreamer into consideration. Nevertheless there are some symbols that point to a possible psychosis, particularly when the symbol often recurs. Tidal waves or other overpowering natural catastrophes point to the fact that a person's consciousness is in danger of being inundated by the unrestrained power of the unconscious. Here is an example:

> I'm standing on the beach; a huge wave is coming toward me. I can't move and I know that it's the end.

This was the dream of a young girl the day before a psychotic episode that had been coming on for more than a year; however, the family had not wanted to see it. Upon admission to the mental hospital the girl said, "I feel as if I don't exist anymore; everything is so far away—I'm sitting on the bottom of the ocean, overwhelmed by the weight of the water."

We often think of dreams as being illogical, confused and absurd, when this is not at all the case. When we dream about a situation that would seem absurd or crazy in reality, the dream often really does reveal a "crazy" situation that is a problem to us at the moment. For example, a catatonic patient wrote down the following dream:

> A street full of people. There is a man who is eight stories tall. He is winding up all the people. They run around like automatons. Then they stand still until the man winds them up again.

Another situation:

> I'm beating a dog like crazy. He's been dead a long time, but I keep on beating him over and over again.

If we were to come upon this latter situation either in reality or in a dream, we would consider it disturbed.

A less dramatic but equally significant form of psychosis is the apathetic withdrawal from reality. What we observe in the patient is expressed even more strongly in dreams that bring shocking images of people dismembered in auto accidents and the like, without the dreamer, either in the dream or upon waking, showing an appropriate reaction.

In most of the dreams mentioned so far, there was no sign of psychosis. In the dream of the extraverted and introverted couple, the fear of wild animals is inappropriate. Had there really been wild animals in the pasture, the dreamer's flight up into the tower would have been an appropriate reaction.

One could not even call the dream of the woman neurotic. It only shows that she is too dependent on status symbols. A clear example of a neurotic dream is that of the woman who compulsively has to make sure through the night that her children were covered up. The inner detached attitude to the children, the indifference that she feels toward them in reality and in the dream borders on the psychotic, but is still in the realm of the neurotic because she is able to relate to what is happening there.

A normal person with problems grapples with dreams that are unmistakably different from dreams that represent neuroses and psychoses. Dreams bring up unconscious material that should become conscious in order to be integrated. The dream's attempt to establish an inner balance (the homeostatic function of the dream) is a part of the normal growth process and is not neurotic.

In dreams as well as in reality, one can separate the "normal" or psychologically healthy person from the neurotic or psychologically ill person by the attitude to the dreamed or actual life situations. Does the person view them as catastrophes or as problems to be solved? If the latter, there is hope.

4
The Dream as a Barometer for the Counselor

After the diagnosis, the actual treatment begins. Let's assume that John and I agree that both partners are able to profit from counseling—either alone or in a group. Dreams remain the best source of information and become the core of the treatment. Gradually the partners learn to understand and to interpret their dreams.

By the way, it is always easier to interpret the dream of another person than one's own. Two people in an intimate relationship can often help each other to understand messages from the unconscious. Indeed, this new common interest may be the first step of a new way of being together. In the beginning, when the individuals are hostile toward each other, they often use the dream as a weapon. Because the dream always points out the unresolved problem, the still undifferentiated function, it is easy to be critical of the other's negative side. At this point, it is again necessary to point out that the dream must be understood in a positive way.

It is also important to look at dreams as a reaction to the therapy: to see how the patient digested the previous session. The therapist can't learn too soon to be open to direct or indirect criticism from the client. Patients do not thereby lose respect for the therapist; in fact, the opposite is the case. They are used to seeing people in authority acting like demi-gods, never admitting a mistake, so it is refreshing to meet someone who can say, "Judging by the dream, it seems that I made you angry in the last session," or "Apparently I got something wrong. Perhaps you can help us both figure out what it was." This generally calls forth good feelings and gives patients confidence in the good intentions of the counselors. They don't feel so inept, infantile and criticized.

A young woman who could not accept much confrontation told me a dream that portrayed some of her shadow sides in creative images and with classical beauty. I was enthusiastic about the dream and completely forgot how unpleasant it would be to her to be faced with all that. I interpreted the dream with great élan and brought an amount of convincing proof to the effect that she wasn't rolling around in the mud anymore. (That was an image from an earlier dream.) Rather, she had come to a new and cleaner way of life (children were playing with sand and water on the beach). I analyzed the dream fully, animated by the colorful material. As she left I thought how happy she must be to have such a clever therapist. I was elated the whole day long.

How great was my disappointment when she arrived for her next session with the following dream. It was very short.

> I'm having dinner at my mother's house. She stuffs big pieces of fried chicken into my mouth. I almost choke. Even before I can swallow, she stuffs an even bigger piece into my mouth. I'm getting nauseous and have to throw up, but she doesn't even notice and keeps feeding me. Finally, as I am leaving, she gives me yet another piece of chicken to take with me.

"I woke up furious at my mother," she said, "and furious at myself for allowing her to overwhelm me like that."

Her words struck me and I realized how wrong I had been. I knew that I could not just work with this dream on the subjective level. I must admit honestly that I was the dream mother who overfed her. When I told her that, she was shocked. Then she admitted that she didn't want to tell me I had overwhelmed her in the last session. She had noticed how happy I was that I could reveal so much to her and how well I had meant it. She didn't want to spoil my happiness. She thought she was a bad person because she had feelings other than gratitude toward me. Besides that she became conscious of her greed—she never had enough; she always wanted more than she could deal with, and she devoured anything that I or someone else gave her without criticism.

On the subjective level she, herself, was the mother who stuffed her, just as she was the person who became nauseous. I freely admitted that I had not been conscious of overfeeding her. I had believed, just like her mother, the more chicken, the better. She didn't hold my blindness against me and was glad that I could accept her reaction. Without the dream, I would never have known what I had done.

In this case, the mistake was not so serious. Naturally every counselor, every therapist, makes mistakes that are not so harmless and can sometimes have far-reaching consequences. However, if one constantly uses the dream as a barometer, one can be somewhat more courageous in counseling than would otherwise be the case. If one is on the wrong track, the dream exerts control by giving a warning. On the other hand, the dream provides confirmation for work that is moving in the right direction.

Sometimes the dream functions not only as a barometer but also as a kind of detective. In the case of Hanna and Eric, there was much that was secret, topics never mentioned. Without dreams, who knows whether their secret would ever have been revealed?

Hanna and Eric appeared at their first session with their pet—a greyhound. If it is true that a dog mirrors the psychological characteristics of its owner, then one could not expect much masculinity from Eric. The couple had hardly entered the room before the dog slid under the table with his tail between his legs. The dog clearly belonged to the man and had an exaggerated place in his life. For example, Hanna said that when the dog was lying on her bed and she wanted to go to sleep, Eric wouldn't let her wake him.

"I can hardly believe that," said John, my co-therapist.

"Why not?" asked Eric, defensively, "a dog also has a right to sleep."

I too was amazed and asked myself whether the man might have a closer relationship with his dog than with his wife, but I thought it too soon to ask as much.

I used the following weeks to get an impression of the couple. Hanna wanted a separation from Eric, but not necessarily a divorce. He was afraid of a separation. He seemed the weaker and more dependent of the two. Gentler than his wife, by profession he was an interior decorator. He had a delicate build and seemed to be sensitive, intuitive and talented. Hanna was more robust and guided by intellect rather than by feelings. She greatly enjoyed her work as a doctor's assistant.

I noted earlier that anima/animus problems often lead to complications in a relationship. With Eric and Hanna it looked as if the animus qualities of the wife and the anima functions of the husband contributed to their problems. I was curious to hear their dreams.

Eric was the first to tell a dream. It was short but gave us much material:

> The dog is very sick. It has silverfish and could possibly die.

Eric said that it was natural for him to dream about the dog. We had already spoken about it several times.

"I had the feeling that you were on my wife's side," he said, "when I said the dog shouldn't be awakened because it was sleeping on the bed. Maybe the dream is saying I'm afraid you might take the dog away from me."

John said, "I can assure you that we don't intend to take your dog away. But what do silverfish mean to you? As far as I know, silverfish are not found in dogs."

Eric explained that silverfish are a kind of vermin that attack wet clothes, old rugs, etc. All kinds of things can be destroyed by it.

In general dogs, as well as other animals in dreams, represent the instinctive side of the dreamer. Dogs are indiscriminate in their sexual behavior, and may mate with breeds other than their own. So they are symbols of promiscuity. These thoughts led me to ask Eric and Hanna about the sexual side of their marriage.

"Nothing," said Hanna morosely, "for a long time, nothing." Eric nodded, ashamed.

John said gently, "We all go through times when we have problems with impotence."

"That's not even it," said Hanna bitterly. "He just doesn't care for me anymore. Our marriage has been unhappy for years."

John asked Eric, "What does this dog mean to you?"

Eric replied, "I never liked dogs when I was young—how they lick themselves and other dogs, always sniffing everything. That was disgusting. But this dog belonged to a friend of mine. It belonged to both of us. It was like our child."

He was near tears and Hanna cleared her throat.

"Did you have a homosexual relationship with the friend you lived with?" I asked.

"Only in the beginning. Later it became a friendship."

"And now?"

"You mean do I still see my former friend? No—we've completely drifted apart."

John said, "The dog in the dream is sick. This represents a lack of a healthy instinctive side of you. And it is infested with vermin."

Eric was silent.

"Do you currently have any kind of homosexual relationship?—anything that is unacceptable to you?"

Eric was not as surprised by the question as I would have thought. He was embarrassed, but was calm as he said, "Homosexual relationships? Nothing of the sort happens around here."

John didn't let up. He had a feeling he was close to "the secret." "You mean that you do not have any homosexual contacts now?"

Eric was silent and suddenly appeared to lose his composure. I said, "It's probably hard for you to talk in your wife's presence."

Hanna interjected, "Eric himself told me about his former homosexual contacts, first in school. Later there was something at the university and, of course, in the army." John remarked that all of that lay back in the past and he was more interested in the present.

Eric was obviously struggling with himself, which surprised Hanna. Suddenly he spoke, very softly and hesitantly. "Sometimes I go to the movies alone. I make contact with men off and on, but it's always very fast and superficial. Afterward I feel guilty."

"Did you know about this?" asked John, turning to Hanna. She shook her head. She was close to tears but pulled herself together.

Eric said, "I couldn't bring myself to confess it to Hanna."

For a moment silence reigned. I noticed how much stronger Hanna was, how much more animus she had compared with Eric's masculinity. She was typical of the strong woman who takes on a soft, sensitive man and later blames him for not being stronger.

And Eric . . .? He was probably the opposite: attracted at first by her strength and self-confidence, and later repelled by her domineering manner and lack of feeling.

Finally she said: "The dog belonged to his friend. He gave him to us as a remembrance of the time when he lived with Eric."

"It would be awful if he died," said Eric, "the dog, I mean."

"Are you still attached to your friend?" I asked Eric.

"Not really," he said, "I'm more attached to the memory; but I don't want to go back to that life." It sounded convincing.

Eric was the type of man we call anima-identified. He was motivated by his feelings to the point where he was partly overrun by sentimentality. Even his work was largely influenced by the nature of his anima. He had a feeling for color and texture, with a strong aesthetic sense. These characteristics had made things tough for him growing up. It had been hard to hold his own against his more athletic and robust classmates, whom he partly admired. He had become attracted to a certain boy who seemed to understand him and that had become his first homosexual relationship.

When he met Hannah he projected his masculine side onto her strongly developed animus. He was happy that she appreciated his gentleness and his artistic talents, and that she wasn't upset by his lack of interest in the everyday concerns of life such as auto repairs. All the things that seemed difficult to him came easy to her. However, their feelings for each other had gradually changed. She reacted to the negative aspects of his anima: his sentimentality, hypersensitivity and self-absorption. He focused on the negative sides of her animus: lack of feeling, a domineering manner and cool objectivity. A great distance had opened up between them.

Hannah's dream at this time showed where she stood inwardly:

I'm going down into a subway; it is dark. I'm on the tracks and a train comes racing toward me. I press myself up against the wall. The train passes so close that I'm in great danger of being ripped to pieces. However, I have no reaction—no fear. When the train has passed, I continue to wander down the tracks. Then a tall strong man appears, picks me up like a child and carries me piggyback up some stairs that lead to the platform. Without saying anything he carries me to the end of the platform. There is an exit to the street. Although he has helped me, I don't like him—I don't trust him. Even so, I want to thank him, but he has already disappeared. I wonder whether we had been invisible since none of the other people on the platform had noticed.

Her associations to the subway were as follows: "I travel by subway to many lectures. I've developed many outside interests because I hate just sitting around the house—we're always fighting. That's why I'm always rushing about from one place to another."

John asked whether this way of life was as dangerous as the train in the subway—and just as mechanical.

She said yes and added, "I know that it is somehow empty to live this way. It's neither healthy nor fulfilling. Sometimes I've thought about death, even suicide, but somehow I'm against that."

Then in her dream the intellect appears—the strong man whom she doesn't like, but who brings her up into the light of day, into daily life. But she wasn't happy always just to "function" and to be praised for it. Her animus, her feeling for responsibility, her common sense, her ability to do what was necessary, carried her through this difficult time. But these qualities didn't mean anything to her anymore. She'd had her fill of always having to function well and to plod along like a good pack animal.

Hannah asked Eric why he had kept his visits to the movies secret.

"It's childish," he said, "but having a secret gave me the feeling of being strong."

"Children keep secrets from their parents for the same reason," she said. From the tone of her voice, it was clear that she wanted to hurt Eric with this remark.

I asked her whether she was aware of how sarcastic her remark was and tried to bring her to the point of expressing her feelings directly instead of attacking him indirectly. That was hard for her, but finally she could admit that Eric's behavior caused her pain. Over many weeks of therapy Hannah learned to acknowledge her feelings and to express them directly instead of grumbling and hiding behind sarcastic comments. During this time she dreamed:

> I am ten years old and living at home with my parents. My father and my older brother were finding fault with me, as had often been the case. I cried and said, "Leave me alone!" They both laughed and left the house. I ran after them and screamed, "I hate you, I hate you!" Then I woke up.

This dream showed how much she still suffered from rejections in early childhood and the extent to which achievement had become the means to gain recognition, first at home and later from men and life in general. She had refused to give in to her feelings and was at first delighted that Eric could express his feelings so freely, that he could allow himself to enjoy playing and following his artistic inclinations—all those things she didn't allow herself. But now she was criticizing Eric for just those things that had delighted her about him at first! He went swimming several times a week; in the summer he played tennis. He had hoped that she would share these things with him. Instead she tried to spoil his fun. Lately he had taken to bicycling on Sunday mornings, which she thought was ridiculous.

Eric started to gain strength from expressing his needs and wishes instead of having secrets and doing things that were not permitted. His dreams showed us that we were on the right track. Dogs and silverfish dreams were our barometer for many months. Again and again sick dogs appeared. But sometimes there were also healthy newborn puppies. Then Eric would regress; he would become anxious and furtive, and animals with silverfish would be back in his dreams.

Even though the therapy was progressing well, Eric was often discouraged. He complained that everything was going too slowly. "The dreams don't say anything." Then came this:

I dreamed I was in Central Park at a much younger age. I have a very lively puppy that is playing with other dogs. I'm sitting in the grass and am so happy, as I haven't been in a long time. Suddenly my father is there and says, "You should be ashamed of yourself! Sitting here like a lazybones! Come home at once and do your homework!" I'm not afraid of him and stay where I am. "I'm staying here," I say. I can hear him saying, "You should be ashamed, killing time like this . . ." but he has disappeared and the words fade away also.

"Congratulations!" I said. "That sounds wonderful."

Eric himself was amazed at the dream. When John asked him whom the father reminded him of, since his father had been dead for a long time, Eric replied at once, "Hannah is just like that. She always tries to make me feel guilty and to spoil what gives me pleasure." Then he turned to her and asked, "Why do you do that? Why don't you ever share anything with me? All you do is complain about me and try to make me feel small."

Hannah retorted, "Well, you never do what I want either! All you ever do is talk about your work and all the things that went wrong during the day. You don't help me with the housework either. I feel like your maid."

Clearly there was still much misunderstanding on both sides, but they talked about it now both during and outside of counseling sessions. The therapy progressed well. However, it wasn't easy for Hannah to move from "spoiling pleasure" to "giving pleasure." Spoiling pleasure made her feel powerful. The price she paid was self-reproach and anxiety that she would lose Eric. She had to learn that power games and true strength are opposites. In the long run, true strength would give her more security than the power games she played out of insecurity. In the midst of the conflict—"How can I become stronger and yet not dominate Eric?"—she had a dream that suggested a simple solution:

I meet a man whom I don't know. We're the same age. He's very vital and masculine, and, at the same time, friendly and warm. There's a kind of radiance about him. I fall in love with him. I'm amazed that he notices me and invites me to sing a duet with him. I tell him that I can't sing at all, but he encourages me to try. I'm afraid of making myself seem ridiculous, but I trust him and try it. We sing a duet and I sing so freely and beautifully that I can hardly believe it's really me. I'm more elated than I have ever been, and I only wish that I could always sing like that and never have to stop.

Hannah said, "Even after I woke up, I was in a unique, elevated mood. But then I became very sad that I can't sing, and that I don't know such a man, and that the whole thing was only a dream."

On the subjective level the man stood for a new, until now unknown, animus attitude. (Heretofore her animus was interested in dominating or was weak and inferior.) This new animus, acquired during weeks of painstaking therapeutic work, invited her to a duet; something shared that led to a complete and harmonious melody. Each voice had its own task; first one led, then the other. They were equal. As far as their marriage was concerned, the realization of this new animus quality meant that Hannah's strength could now be a complement to what Eric had to "sing"—to say in life.

The result of the therapy was a new beginning, a new relationship and an awakening of long dormant sexual interest. They had their first sexual experience together after months of abstinence and both felt that that was a high point. They believed that all of their problems had been solved. Then the dog cropped up again in one of Eric's dreams. It looked old, tired and was infested with silverfish. This time there was no secret. After the night making love with Hannah, Eric had gone once again to the movies in order to assure himself, he said, that he would no longer succumb to any kind of temptation. However, he did succumb to the attraction of the forbidden situation. He was badly shaken by this experience and believed that he hadn't made any progress at all, that he was a hopeless case.

Eric and Hannah had outgrown the sterility of the fighting stage of their relationship and were now ready for group therapy with other couples.

5
The Role of Dreams in Group Therapy

A major benefit of group therapy is that partners see that they are not the only ones who have problems. Frequently a man will think, "If I had married someone like Mrs. X, everything would have worked out much better." In the group he finds out that Mr. and Mrs. X have just as much tension on account of their differences, their expectations of each other and their projections as do he and his wife.

Often people are more willing to accept a confrontation from a member of a group than from the marriage counselor. For example, it is fortunate when a wife sees that another woman in the group really likes her husband and doesn't find his negative sides so damnable. It is also the case that a man benefits from being confronted by another man in the group instead of by his wife or a female therapist. In general, the group offers understanding, shares common problems, and supports the person who is disheartened, or rebuffs those who expect too much attention.

In a group one learns how others perceive one and what must change in order to achieve better relations with others. Some people talk too much, some too little; some are shy, others too brusque. Each of us has a shadow side. In a group the shadow is activated and then worked through with the help of the group. This process is a big support for each member of the group.

The group Hannah and Eric joined consisted of three couples who hadn't worked together very long. They had only just begun to feel like a single unit with a sense of belonging. The group had just been discussing Martin's premarital relationships. Martin, a twenty-six-year-old biochemist, had been married to Hilda for two years. Hilda, twenty-two, had been a laboratory assistant. In her eighth month of pregnancy she had recently quit her job.

The original reason for their marital difficulties was problems with

65

the in-laws such as differing views on obligations and the like. Although these conflicts had for the most part resolved themselves, a burdensome new problem had emerged. Martin was so "married" to his work that he had hardly any time for his wife. In previous meetings of the group, this had led to discussion of his leisure-time activities and the women in the group brought this up again. Now Martin had come with a dream, which he wanted to share with the group:

> A vibrant, natural young woman from the country leads me to an old romantic European city. She brings me to an old tower and we climb all the way to the top. We have a wonderful time there. It is unbelievably romantic. We are completely in love with each other and we make love. When it is time to leave, she suddenly throws herself out of the window. For a long moment I think that she has killed herself, but when I look out I see her flying happily around the tower. She beckons me to follow her. I do and now both of us are flying over the delightful landscape. I woke up with such a happy feeling.

At once a lively discussion broke out in the group.

Clark (a worldly television producer of a literary evening program; forty years old, with a smug façade, although quite weak underneath): "Here you have your earthy child of nature—isn't your laboratory assistant such a creature?"

Leslie (twenty years old, Clark's former secretary, now his wife; a somewhat naive young woman from the Midwest, a very natural type of person): "What do you mean by that?"

Clark: "Are you playing naive again?"

Elli (also twenty, often identified with Leslie; likewise rather naive, shy, prudish; she has sexual problems with her husband Tom, who is also very young): "Leave your wife alone!"

Tom: "I hate this kind of nattering. It doesn't get us anywhere."

Renée (me, counselor): "Do you have a positive suggestion?"

Tom: "Hilda is so different from the women Martin usually talks and dreams about. I have to ask myself (turning to Hilda, Martin's wife) how she feels when she hears all this."

Hilda (an ethereal creature with long limbs, long fingers; a rather fragile type) merely shrugged her shoulders indifferently, evidently not ready to open up to Tom.

John: (co-counselor): "I thought we decided not to ask each other questions, but to say what we mean. Obviously Hilda doesn't feel like answering your questions. Tom, can you tell us what your feelings are and what it means to you to know what Hilda is feeling?"

Tom: "It means a lot to me. I like Hilda. Somehow I have the feeling that I have to protect her."

Martin: "From me?"

Tom nods: "You don't seem to appreciate her at all."

Martin: "How can you say that? I do appreciate Hilda—I love her. I never wanted to marry such a free spirit; otherwise I would have done so. Hilda is intelligent and creative. She never talks about it, but she should bring her drawings to show us sometime. She's also musical. We're really suited to each other, and that is much more important to me than any free spirit who loves nature; a woman only good to spend time with outdoors, but not for living with day after day."

Clark: "Hear! Hear!"

Leslie (very angry): "Well, that's really charming—thanks for the compliment!"

Elli: "Don't even answer him!"

Hilda: "I don't think that the meaning of this dream can be found on the objective level. It seems to me that it has to do with something in Martin himself—an inner conflict, but I don't understand the dream well enough to be able to say something about it."

John: "The two of you aren't even talking to each other. You're only talking about each other. Have you ever noticed that? First you, Martin, describe your wife as if she weren't even in the room and now you, Hilda, talk about the dream as if Martin weren't here."

Hilda: "Yes, strange, isn't it? Martin, what do you think this romantic anima figure is all about? She must be somehow a part of yourself. I still remember you like that, but it was a long time ago."

Martin: "Yes, a long time ago. I've always had a real need to be out in nature. But more and more I've been burying myself in my laboratory—all day, nights, weekends—always work.

Tom: "Are you that bound up in your work? Don't you get tired?"

Martin: "I'm practically obsessed with my work."

Hilda: "That's why you don't allow yourself to have free time."

Martin: "But since we've been talking about this I've become more and more conscious that I need something different, some balance. It's very much like the dream says."

Clark: "Yes, you must allow yourself more free time to get out into nature. That is more important than being with a free spirit."

Martin: "I'm glad you said that. I'm glad you understand. I know that Hilda . . . (turning to his wife) that you are the right wife for me, but I have to fit the side of me that loves nature into my life more. Right now I feel so far away from the dream. I feel heavy, like a block of wood, completely inert, without anima, much less one that can fly."

Renée: "Can you imagine anything that you could do that would give you such a feeling of elation?"

Martin: "If only I could climb a mountain, go hiking for a few hours—ah! (stretching both arms out wide) then I'd feel young again. Yes, that would be like flying."

Hanna: "What's stopping you?"

Martin: "I am—I have to change something in my life."

In the next session I turned to Hilda and said, "Last time when the group was talking to Martin about his free spirit, it seemed to me that you were getting quite nervous."

Clark: "What did you dream about after the last meeting?"

Hilda: "Not much—my aunt was snooping about in the attic."

Clark: "Is that all?"

Tom: "Could you tell us something about your aunt? How old she is, what her name is, what she looks like?"

Hilda: "I don't think that would help, but I've been wrong before. How old she is—I don't know—she's no longer alive. She was really very nice. We called her Aunt Neil . . ."

Tom: "Aunt Neil!" (Everyone laughs.)

Hilda (confused): "What's so funny?"

Clark: "Could there be a connection between 'Neil' and 'Nell'?"

Hilda (surprised): "Perhaps . . . I didn't think of it."

The discussion about the "snooping" therapist took a completely different turn than we had expected. The tension that Hilda felt while Martin talked about his premarital relationships had nothing to do with jealousy. On the contrary. When all the associations and recollections had come out, it turned out that Hilda was afraid that I would also ask her about her premarital relationships. She would not feel comfortable talking freely in her husband's presence, she said, because he was much more jealous about her past than she was about his. These thoughts had been going through her head while her husband was working on his dream and they had made her anxious.

Indeed, Martin's excessive jealousy was causing problems in the marriage, which were hardly bearable. Martin was aware how difficult it was for Hilda to live with his jealousy. On the other hand, she knew how agonizing it was for Martin not to be able to do anything to change the situation.

The group asked questions about his childhood.

"I came down with polio when I was about twelve years old," Martin said. "I made a good recovery, but for years I couldn't play sports. I felt inferior to the other kids and even the girls treated me like a second-class citizen. I couldn't dance, so naturally I didn't get many invitations to parties—oh! It was so hard!"

He grew quiet and looked very sad. It became clear that he had felt quite inferior in his masculinity during his adolescence and thus was hypersensitive and over-anxious around girls. He felt that other boys were competing against him when they weren't. He feared rejection even when there were no grounds for it.

John said, "Now I understand why you bury yourself in your work. If you can't dance, then in all other areas it's as if you were saying, 'I'll show them!' " Martin looked at John gratefully. He felt understood and nodded in agreement. He said that even though he had received much recognition for his work at his age, still his jealousy had unfortunately not diminished. Now he felt that somehow the group had opened a door for him. The confrontations by the group members, their understanding, their good feelings toward him, the empathetic remarks—all these gave him the hope that perhaps one day the problems that stemmed from his childhood could be overcome.

"It helps to talk so openly," said Martin. "Before I was always so ashamed about these things—as well as over problems that developed with impotence. I didn't even want to talk about it with Hilda. Now things don't seem so terrible and painful. I feel much better!"

It often happens that long-hidden or half-forgotten problems will suddenly come out in the group. Their disclosure can lead to a good solution. However, that isn't always the case. The revealing of earlier experiences does not provide a sense of relief for some people, but is painful and burdensome, causing hostility toward the group and its leader, as well as the very idea of group therapy. The individual may simply stop coming without any explanation.

On the other hand, other participants remain in the group while trying to keep their problems to themselves.

Clark was such a person. He constantly encouraged others to speak openly about themselves. He was always prepared to confront others and also to support them when necessary. He acted as if he were the group leader and the others often teased him about it. However, gradually the group began to resent Clark for so cleverly avoiding all confrontation, especially since his wife, Leslie, was unhappy and wanted a discussion of their problems.

No one really knew what their problems were. Only one thing was obvious to everyone: their age difference. Clark was forty years old, had lived with many women, but had not married before Leslie. He had traveled widely. He was worldly wise, highly intellectual, witty, and frequently sarcastic. He had been a sought-after bachelor, surrounded by women who would gladly have married him. Moreover he was a creative and well-known television producer who moved with ease in the world of beautiful women and prominent men.

Leslie was from the Midwest and had become Clark's secretary as soon as she arrived in New York. She was twenty years old, very pretty and intelligent. She had an unspoiled natural manner about her, which was unusual in Clark's circle. He fell in love with this beautiful young woman. He took her to the theater and backstage to meet the actors. He gave her books to read which he then discussed with her. He took her to nightclubs, which was something new to her. She was his discovery and he was completely in the thrall of this Pygmalion romance.

It wasn't clear what he wanted to make out of Leslie. In any case, she was dazzled by the brilliance of his personality, by his money, and by their lifestyle. And she was overwhelmed when he asked her to marry him after only a short time. His motives were self-seeking, although Leslie wasn't aware of this at the time. He wanted to impress his friends with his beautiful young wife, and prove to himself that he could make her into the wife who would make life pleasant for him. In addition, he hoped so to bind her to him sexually that he would never lose her. For Leslie the idea of becoming Clark's wife was a dream come true. Her only fear was that she didn't have enough to offer and so didn't deserve him.

Clark had been coming to me for therapy long before he married Leslie. His dreams showed him in a completely different light than Leslie's perspective. A couple of short but typical dreams show what his problems were.

> I'm sitting with Leslie in the studio, showing her a film I've made. The film looks more significant than others I've made and it means a success for me. Leslie is sitting in front of me. Ellen is behind me. I have vindictive feelings toward Ellen. It serves her right that my film is so successful and, moreover, that I'm engaged to be married to Leslie. I would like so much to know what Ellen is feeling. When a seat next to Leslie becomes available, I move there, not so much to sit near Leslie, but to make Ellen jealous.

In Clark's dreams women always appear who cannot be analyzed as individuals. The relationships function is a kind of role-play or they have some other secondary consideration. On the subjective level it turned out that Clark used, even prostituted, his own feelings in superficial ways. As for the rest of his life, he had problems with his work as a writer. He was disappointed about this because he had the ambition to become famous. So far he had not succeeded in this. Either his books weren't completed or they were too superficial to be accepted by a publisher. Everything was always just appearance—like the film in his dream, which he considered his success although it remained an open question whether it was even his film.

Another dream showed the problem from another side.

> I want to show one of my films to the directors, but suddenly it's only a piece of a film, then it's part of a novella—it's unclear just what it is. The actors are dressed up as animals. I think that is a brilliant idea; I don't know why. However, all in all, the production is disappointing. My girl-friend, who wanted to see the production, has disappeared. Everyone has left the theater. The presentation is broken off. A man comes up to me and says, "This always happens with our company. Everything is arranged for the performance, but nobody stays until the end. Everything remains incomplete. Nothing is ever finished!"

Originally Clark had begun therapy because he thought he had writer's block. As the above-mentioned dream points out, he already saw himself as the author sitting at the performance even before the piece was completed. Clark didn't have writer's block in the usual sense at all, but was so preoccupied with his daydreams of success that he could seldom actually get down to the tedious work of writing. Everything had to be different and original, but he lacked thoroughness.

This last dream ended in a typical way for Clark:

> Dan, one of the directors, didn't like my film. He said the piece was effective, but not clear or concise enough. I mumbled something and leaned forward to tie my shoelaces. Then Dan unexpectedly rubbed my neck in a playful way. I thought to myself that perhaps I could win him over to my film if I were to begin a homosexual flirtation with him.

During the time Clark was playing with the idea of marrying Leslie, I had warned him, for his sake as well as for hers, saying that, as far as I could tell, Leslie could be greatly wounded in a marriage with him. It seemed to me that his motives for marrying her were superficial and dishonest. I didn't see how he could justify marrying this naive young woman. He was offended by my question as to which role he would be in as he approached the marriage. Following that session he dreamed:

> I'm sitting at a table with Ed; it's not Ed as he is now, but as an old man. Renée is there, but she is not herself either. Has Ed turned into Renée? Lou is there, but not as Lou. He's a famous star from the well-known novel by Harris. Or maybe he is there as my father.

This part of the dream exposes Clark's lack of identity in a shocking way. No one is as he or she really is. Everyone is mixed up with everyone else. How can he know which of the many Clarks is going to marry Leslie? The dream continues:

> I'm speaking in public and I direct my remarks to a certain woman in the audience. The situation is similar to the therapy sessions with Renée, but then again, not really. My memory of what I said changes constantly and is full of contradictions. On the one hand, I feel I've presented myself in a manly way and that I've been brilliantly effective in presenting my topic. On the other hand, I feel that I'm just using this manliness as a pose. I even say that I have no idea what I'm feeling. My friends, especially Renée, have the impression that I'm just bragging about my manliness and showing off. Are they undermining me? Or are they showing me how badly I've behaved in a way that would be constructive for me? I assume that no one is rejecting me and that, in fact, they like me very much. However, I decide to do nothing until everything becomes more clear.

Clark dreamed this in regard to the question why he wanted to marry Leslie and who in him wanted to marry her. Poor Leslie didn't yet see how hollow her hero was, how insecure he was in his identity and masculinity. In this last part of the dream the point was not what he did to be more masculine. He was only preoccupied with impressing others or to find out if the others could see through him. He hadn't achieved anything that would have been a real expression of manliness. Words, many words, and behind them? —an anxious void.

This was the last session before my summer vacation. I had recently become acquainted with Leslie and had the feeling that she had no idea what was in store for her in a marriage with Clark. I tried to warn her as much as I could. Clark was there. He made witty remarks to everything I said about him. It was clear to me that they would not follow my advice to wait a while before getting married.

When I returned from vacation, they were married and the problems had already begun. Leslie came alone to see me with a list of questions, behind which lay doubt and disappointment.

"Is it true," she asked, "that all married men have mistresses? Is it really being bourgeois not to want to go to bed with him and another woman? Is my desire to go to college a 'modern misunderstanding'? How can I find out whether I'm stupid or intelligent?"

The questions showed clearly where the problems were in this marriage. It was crucial that Leslie's questions be answered quickly. I advised both of them to start group therapy, preferably with a group of ordinary folks, not people from the world of movies and television.

Clark smirked at this idea and replied arrogantly, "And you think that will do Leslie some good?"

I made no bones about the fact that he needed the group as much as Leslie did, if not more.

"Okay," he said in a cool manner, "Maybe I can get some interesting material for my next screenplay."

After this go-round Leslie was amazed that Clark said so little in the group and was satisfied with merely giving others advice. This behavior was exactly what I had expected. He played his cards close to the chest and hid his anxiety behind a façade of the intelligent, worldly, experienced man. I let him have his way, for I assumed that the group would soon become impatient with him and would press him to let down his guard. This moment had indeed arrived.

Leslie started crying and the group encouraged her to talk. Clark paid no attention to Leslie's tears and continued puffing away on his pipe. The group asked Leslie if she'd like to talk. She nodded.

John asked, "Do you want to say anything, Clark?"

Clark: "Me? What gives you that idea?"

Leslie: "All right—if you won't say anything, then I'll talk. We've been sitting here for weeks afraid to say anything."

Clark laughed sarcastically, but Leslie continued, "I want to tell you about my dream last night. I only have nightmares, dreams in which I am either crying or I've died—it's so terrible!"

Hilda (who sat next to Leslie, reached over to touch her hand): "Tell us your dream. Maybe it will make you feel a little better."

No one knew why Leslie was so unhappy. Her dream told us:

> I dreamed that Clark left me. I felt so lonely and was in a daze. Although Clark had been unhappy and depressed lately and was disappointed in our marriage, still, I never thought he would leave me. I started crying. Then the telephone rang. It was Joy. She said that she was with Clark in his old apartment. That news went through me like a knife. I wanted to strangle both of them, especially Joy. She said that Clark was drunk and she was taking care of him. "Well, take care of him then!" I said, angrily.
>
> Clark got on the phone. He sounded drunk. He said he wanted to stay with Joy for a while. He laughed. I thought he was laughing at me, at himself, at the whole world! I was hurt and completely beside myself. He always goes away from me when he's unhappy. Why? He's definitely unhappy with me. That's why he left. He goes to Joy so that she can console him. To hell with both of them!

Hanna wanted to know what had happened the day before.

Leslie: "Oh, the usual—Joy appeared again unexpectedly for dinner and she and Clark were like two peas in a pod, as usual."

Ellie: "Who is Joy?"

Leslie: "His former mistress. She wants to be my best friend. Clark told her that she can come over whenever she wants, that she should consider herself part of the family. At first I thought that was great, but now I hate it more and more."

Hilda: "Why?"

Leslie: "She pokes her nose into everything. I showed her my new dress. It was inexpensive, but so simple and pretty. She only laughed, looked at Clark, and said, 'I think we should show Leslie how to dress.' 'Yes,' said Clark, 'I'll give you money to take her shopping—she can learn a lot from you.' "

John: "Is that the way it happened, Clark?"

Clark: "Yeah, I guess so. Does that seem strange?

Tom: "Are you being serious?"

Renée: "It seems that you haven't given a thought to how your wife feels about the situation."

Clark: "She told me she'd enjoy going shopping with Joy."

Leslie (in a loud, accusing voice): "What was I supposed to do, cry? I wanted to scream, 'Throw her out! Clark, why don't you go shopping with me? You always went shopping with her.' But what was I supposed to do?"

Martin: "I'm a very modern man, but even I think this situation is going a bit too far."

Hilda: "I bet this is usual behavior in Clark's circle."

Leslie: "No, only with a few people—most of the marriages are quite normal. Former lovers don't come to the house and aren't considered part of the family."

Ellie: "I'd never put up with that."

Clark: "Leslie knew Joy before we got married and has always looked up to her—isn't that right, Baby?"

Leslie: "Don't call me 'Baby'! Yes, I thought Joy would be a good friend and would help me to understand things better."

Clark: "But she does that! —What do you want, anyway?"

Leslie: "She pokes her nose into everything. It's always as if the two of you were married and I'm just your plaything."

Martin (turning to Clark): "Why didn't you marry Joy?"

Clark: "We tried to live together a number of times, but it didn't work. She's too strong for me . . . too much animus. She can do everything, she knows everything, she's always the boss. When we don't live together, then we get along wonderfully!"

Leslie (sarcastically): "Well, that really makes me happy!"

Hanna: "So this Joy woman was at your house the evening before you had the dream—what happened then?"

Leslie: "She whispered to me that she wanted to give Clark a surprise party for his birthday in her apartment next week. I said that I wanted to spend his birthday alone with him, but I wanted Clark to do what he likes to do. Then she spoke to me in that condescending tone that I hate, 'I know what he likes, don't you worry!' I didn't have the nerve to tell her off."

Erich: "Does Clark know how you feel?"

John: "Why don't you ask him directly?"

Clark: "It's all clear—but, after all, it's Leslie's problem if she's jealous, not mine."

Everyone talked at the same time. "That's unbelievable—how could anyone be so cold and indifferent. Don't you care that Leslie is suffering?"

Ellie: "I wouldn't stay married to a man like that."

Leslie: "It's not so easy to be married to me either. There have been nights when I've just cried hysterically. He was furious but didn't say anything."

Renée: "Did you tell him that you were angry too?"

Leslie only shook her head, ashamed.

Ellie: "I think it's unfair that we're reproaching Leslie—it's perfectly clear that Clark is to blame."

Renée: "It's not our job to find out who's guilty."

Tom, very upset: "Does that mean that there's no such thing as right and wrong?"

Hilda: "Certainly not—no one says that."

Tom (in a hostile way): "After all, what's the point of what we're doing here?"

Martin: "To help—to understand—to become aware of what we're doing or not doing and why. Why is Leslie afraid to tell her husband that she's angry? That is much more complex than the question of right or wrong."

Tom: "Clark's behavior is really immoral. It makes me so angry."

John: "Maybe you could say a little more about that. What does it mean to you? Why does it make you angry when someone acts badly or immorally?"

Tom was confused by the question. Naturally it was easier for him to make Clark the scapegoat than to go into the question of his anger over the "sinner." We all find it easier to act like Tom.

Finally Tom got things straightened out with himself and made a confession: "Basically I envy guys like Clark. They're much more gutsy than I am. I'm too shy and awkward to have a mistress, much less to bring her to my house and all that. I have fantasies about such things, but Clark—he does it and even finds a wife who goes along. Yeah, I envy that!"

Then a frank discussion took place that ended with Martin saying, "Clark, we all act like you have much more than the rest of us, just because you have two women in your life, or maybe three. I tried that myself but found out that more women only leads to less in the way of relationship. It was a nice game, but it didn't give me depth of intimacy. It diminished the friendship I had with my wife. I wasn't there for her then—everything was different, superficial."

Eric nodded. "I'm just coming out of such a phase myself," he said. "Now that I no longer allow myself to have flings, Hanna and I have a completely different relationship. I feel that I gained in quality when I gave up quantity."

Leslie: "I like what you're saying."

Clark: "Maybe I'm not as enthusiastic about your 'confrontation' and 'growth' as you are. I find it quite pleasant, when I'm angry with one woman, to then go to another woman to be consoled—even though I'm not becoming 'more mature.' "

Tom: "Now I'm not angry at you anymore. I don't envy you any longer. I feel that you need help and understanding. Perhaps in the process I could learn why I envied you so much at first."

John and I were struck by the fact that, during the time the group worked on the dream, no one was interested in the detail about Clark's being drunk. No one asked if that were true. That points up a decisive difference between dream therapy in a group and in individual treatment.

In group therapy, dreams are frequently used as a springboard for a mutual exchange of feelings and ideas. Each person seizes on what seems most interesting to him or her. That means that the dream is not worked through systematically, unlike what happens in individual therapy. If the dream contains sexual material, the group is usually more interested in that than in a problem like drinking. The counselor has to decide whether he or she will let the confrontation continue for the duration of the discussion, as in Leslie's case, or whether to point out that a crucial part of the dream has not been noticed. In the case of Leslie's dream, we gave the group interaction free play, because it was so productive.

Both of us were aware of the part alcohol played in the life of this couple, and knew that everything connected with it would probably surface soon by itself. The problem of unfaithfulness, the idea of right and wrong, a discussion of a value system in the therapy in general, all seemed more important than a systematic working through of the dream. This was particularly so since this group was made up of people who had not had a lot of individual therapy. Therefore it seemed necessary to explain a few basic concepts.

It is not important to the couple counselor that a dream be understood and worked through in its entirety by the group. It rather serves as a barometer. With the help of dreams one can orient oneself as to where the patient is at the moment: how he or she relates to problems and to the world. For this group the dreams elicited the problems of the various members as follows:

Eric was disturbed in his instinctual sphere because of his secret and unsatisfactory homosexual relations. Hanna, his wife, was fed up with always functioning well and feeling so empty and tired.

Martin, by burying himself in his work, was cut off from his inner feminine side, his longing for the mountains and nature. His wife Hilda was afraid to talk about her past and felt very unhappy.

Clark neither knew who he really was nor what he wanted except for sensual satisfaction. His dream showed him as a person without a responsible value system, without real identity. Leslie was still far from recognizing that the brilliance that had dazzled her came from a fake diamond. Her first dream pointed out her weakness: her seduction by the glitter of the "big world" (symbolized in the dream by the easy-going Joy). The undervaluing of her own strength had led her to accept Clark without criticism.

The couple counselor must consider whether the insights received from a dream should be fully probed in the group. Sometimes it is more appropriate to suggest an individual therapy session. This was the case for Leslie's dream in which Clark is drunk. Clark is the most important animus figure for Leslie. Her own animus is therefore "drunk"—not in a conscious state. Can she understand what that means? The dream's message was clear for my co-therapist John: she had made herself unaware and weakened herself. Her "alcohol" is life in the world of the socially prominent. She is drunk from elegant parties, horse races and so much money.

When and how should John raise this topic? If he is reading the barometer of the dream correctly, then he'll find the right way and the right time to share this information from her own unconscious. In general, one can say that the dreamer is capable of understanding the message of the dream if he or she is dreaming it.

Other questions arise: What other pressing problems are present at the same time in the group? Can other group members learn something about themselves—or gain some general insight—from a deep examination of another group member's dream? For example, Leslie's dream could suggest the questions: "What is *my* alcohol? How do I numb myself? What am I running from?"

As mentioned, it is crucial that the dreamer be strong enough to stand a confrontation over a specific dream in the group. The disclosure of an unpleasant shadow side must usually be broached carefully in an individual session before the problem can be usefully worked on in the group.

The counselor realizes from the dreams whether the person seeking help has made progress, has regressed, or is just going around in circles with the old problems. Hannah's dream of a strong and masculine figure (a positive animus) with whom she sings a duet certainly marks progress over the first dream she told. This was also the case with the healthy puppies in Eric's dreams.

With Clark, on the other hand, it was otherwise. In spite of marriage, individual therapy and group therapy, nothing had changed in his dreams compared with dreams before his marriage. It was always the same theme of shadowy characters that had no identity. The motifs of the action in the dream usually had to do with manipulating or impressing someone. Since he didn't change anything in his life, everything remained the same: his behavior, his symptoms, and his dreams.

When Eric once again relapsed into his old habits, albeit for a short time, the symbol of the silverfish would promptly appear in a dream. On Eric's barometer of meaning, "silverfish" was clearly the sign of shady, problematic behavior. When Eric dreams of silverfish at a time that Hannah sings duets in her dream, the comparison of both dreams allows the counselor to infer how near or far each partner is from the other. The therapy has made real headway when the partners themselves learn to grasp the dream's meaning from the depth of the unconscious instead of merely speculating from each other's behavior as to what is going on with the other person. The realization of the whole situation leads to a completely new and productive dialogue.

With Chuck and Joan (the couple who reacted so differently to the planned party) the dream implied a further possibility of deepening the understanding of the situation. It pointed out the difference in personality type between the two. Now their behavior toward each other as well as toward other people could be seen in a clearer light. Again and again the marriage counselor brought up "typical" behavior of extraverts and introverts, with all the advantages and drawbacks of each. This allowed many previously hostile arguments to be defused with humor.

The analytic "transference" becomes very obvious through dreams.

Group members become aware of how they all project the situation in their childhood homes onto others in the group.

A good example of this is Hilda, who did not want to talk about her premarital relationships and was afraid that I might ask about them. She dreamed of an aunt who was actually very nosy and whose name was similar to mine. When Hannah dreamed of herself as a ten year old who was always criticized by her father and brother, she saw almost all the men in the group, including the counselor, John, as enemies who wanted to belittle her. It was the dream that first clarified for her, as well as for the rest of us, how she suddenly fell into this trap.

The use of dreams in therapy puts an end to fruitless "advice-giving" in counseling. Group members and counselors, who find answers to their questions in dreams, are closer to the truth than those who judge others by themselves or who rely on a mixture of observation, projection or general moral theories for advice. This applies particularly toward the end of couple therapy.

Finally, dreams show when the partners have come far enough to foresee the end of the therapy with confidence. Dreams can also indicate when the decision to terminate therapy has been made prematurely. In this phase, therefore, dreams are a big help. The termination of therapy is often contentious because the couple sometimes wants to stop too soon or sometimes it's the other way around—the counselor thinks the couple could continue to help each other without therapy, but they would rather remain in the group where they feel safe and secure.

6
Dreams as a Guide in the Final Stage of Counseling

The final phase of therapy begins when the counselor and the couple see the end as a possibility. This happens when the partners understand their most important problems and have learned to communicate with each other in a constructive way. These criteria are relevant signposts whether the pair has decided to divorce, to stay together, to go into individual therapy, to separate temporarily, or to stay together on the basis of friendship or until their children are older.

When the partners express the wish to end counseling, I usually suggest that we wait and see how the unconscious will react to the suggestion—to see what the dream will "say" to us. Often the partners have very different dreams because they have different reactions to the idea of ending counseling. Working through these dreams will guide us in deciding whether to continue or terminate the therapy.

As an example I'll mention Erwin, who was not at all happy about coming to his first interview. He refused to consider individual therapy, but was reluctantly prepared to take part in marital group therapy with his wife, Lotte. He discovered that he liked it better than he thought he would. After a few weeks, however, he wanted to stop. The group was skeptical as to whether he had come far enough and advised him to leave the decision to his unconscious. At the next session Erwin brought a dream that revealed the degree to which he was still driven in his life.

My wife and I are in our house which is very spacious. I hear the telephone ringing in the kitchen and go to answer it. Just as I get there, it stops. Another phone starts ringing in the bedroom. I run quickly to answer it. Again it stops ringing before I can get there. I run faster and faster in this way through maybe ten rooms of the house. It's always the same thing: the phone rings and then stops before I can answer it. The last time it rings in the living room and again stops before I reach it. My wife is in the living room. Suddenly the light goes out.

I want to fix it right away, but my wife says, "It's peaceful to sit in the darkness—in the quiet." She asks me to sit beside her. I've hardly sat down for a second when I hear a dog barking outside. I jump up and run outside to see what is happening. Much to my surprise I see the dog barking at the moon—but it isn't just one moon—it's eight moons!

After this dream it was hard for Erwin to maintain that he was steeling himself against outside temptations. He laughed and admitted that eight moons were really seven more than were necessary. He talked about getting some individual therapy himself, in addition to the group sessions, in order to work on the compulsive use of his energy that was causing such wear and tear on himself.

Lotte's dream also led her to reconsider ending her participation in the group:

I'm looking out the window. It's the fall of the year. On the one hand, it's beautiful with colorful leaves and birds flying south, but it's also very melancholy.

"I woke up feeling somewhat depressed," she said.

On account of Erwin's minor heart problems Lotte had begun to consider herself a middle-aged woman. She felt that her "fall" had begun. She no longer saw what was beautiful, only what was depressing—the change of life. In fact, she saw herself as a lonely widow already and she often thought about death. The group was heartfelt in their support and Lotte was happy that she could continue coming.

Meanwhile, much had happened in the group to which Leslie and Clark belonged. Twenty-year-old Elli and her twenty-one-year-old husband Tom had, for the most part, worked out their sexual problems and had come far enough in four months to consider leaving the group. Then Elli brought the following dream:

I'm in bed with my husband when my mother appears and stands at the foot of the bed. She doesn't say anything—she just looks at me reproachfully.

That corresponded to reality. Elli's mother had died long ago, but, unconsciously, Elli brought the taboos that her mother had warned her about into the marriage: Men are animals and sex is a dirty thing. The dream pointed clearly to the problem—for Elli, her mother was not dead. On the contrary, in regard to their married life, her mother was very much alive and present. On the subjective level the mother's voice had become the voice of Elli's conscience. A free and open discussion about the meaning of love, marriage and sexuality took place with those couples that had been married longer. This found a good echo in both Elli's and Tom's dreams. In Elli's dreams, in particular, problems of an unlived adolescence appeared.

> A party—everyone is sixteen years old and wearing pajamas and nighties. There's a lot of necking going on. I feel very young—like a teenager. My husband and I are lying on the couch kissing when my mother appears and says, "I only want to see that everything's ok." I reply, "Why don't you leave us alone!"
>
> Mother didn't go, but when I woke up I felt quite proud of myself for finally speaking my mind.

Elli had never been allowed to go to parties and had just skipped the teenage period when the experiences of flirting, sex and love are so prominent. Ellie and Tom's marriage was not really disturbed, but both were rather inexperienced. Therefore their therapy consisted more in education than in depth therapy. That's why the change in Elli went quickly and smoothly and both could soon leave the group. When Elli and Tom told the group that they were ready to leave, they were also advised to pay close attention to any dreams that occurred. Tom came to the next session with a dream that was typical for the final phase of counseling:

> Elli and I are riding a bicycle-built-for-two. Between us on the bar sits a brand new baby, who looks rather grown-up and can already talk. That didn't seem at all unusual.

Tom said, "But we don't want to have a baby. We haven't even been married a year and we're just starting to understand each other.

Does the dream mean that perhaps I unconsciously want us to have a baby?"

"I don't think so," answered John. "Is there something in your life that feels new, and yet not completely new or helpless?"

"I think it's our marriage," Elli threw out. "When we're both getting along well, there's a feeling that's like riding a bicycle-built-for-two. We're moving in the same direction and everything is good. Sex is like that now too. We're in the same rhythm and I have such a feeling of closeness."

Shortly thereafter Elli told her concluding dream:

> I'm going to a funeral with my sister. I'm in a calm and happy mood and wonder why I'm not more sad. My sister says, "Everybody has to die when their time comes and I believe her time had come." I reply, "But whom are we burying?" "Oh, you don't know yet—we're burying our mother." Without any feeling of shock or guilt I say, "Ah, that's why it's such a beautiful and sunny day."

After she woke up, Elli was astonished and guilty that the death of her mother hadn't shocked her more. After careful consideration Elli agreed with her sister in the dream—it was time finally to let go of her mother who had been dead for years.

Tom was just as satisfied with the progress of the therapy. He had learned to understand his wife and himself better. He was glad that his mother-in-law had not only left the bedroom, but had disappeared from their life. Both thought they would be able to handle their problems on their own.

In Elli and Tom's case the problems were relatively straightforward. Both of them were conscious of the nature of their problems and were willing to speak openly about their sexual dilemma. However, even in this case one needed dreams as a barometer in order to be really sure what Elli must do to develop into a young woman able to enjoy all aspects of her marriage.

Naturally, such a short and successful therapy is not the rule but the exception. It is even an indication that the partners don't need treatment in the true sense of the word, but rather some education and guidance.

With Leslie and Clark the situation was completely different from the very beginning. While I will mostly be presenting their dreams in the final phase, I would also like to describe the development of Clark and Leslie's situation step by step. The dreams will show why their situation led to divorce. (In this connection it is important for me to say that the excerpts of dialogue and group interaction that are concerned with Leslie and Clark could give the impression that the group was concerned exclusively with the two of them. This is not the case. When one thinks that the group discussions lasted an hour and a half at a time, it is clear that the relevant exchanges took up only a part of that time.)

Clark's elegant ways had dazzled Leslie so that she didn't see how degenerate he really was. This can be attributed to her inexperience with men, especially men like Clark and his friends, who lived for pleasure above all. As often as her honesty and clearheaded way of thinking caused her to doubt Clark's lifestyle, he would point out with brilliant logic how bourgeois, childish and inexperienced she still was.

However, as time went on, Leslie secretly doubted the soundness of his arguments more and more. The group was very critical of the unequal aspects of their relationship. One had the impression that Leslie's need for more integrity in her partnership was ignored by Clark, but supported by the group. Gradually Leslie began to see Clark through the group's eyes. The more this process advanced, the more she feared having to make a decision she wasn't ready for: the break-up of her marriage.

Instead of confronting Clark with her doubts, she decided on another solution: she put herself in Clark's place and tried to do everything he did in the hope of seeing things in a different light. Clark drank a lot. Leslie, who didn't drink, had criticized him. Now she began to drink. It didn't agree with her, but she trained herself; indeed, she compelled herself to do it.

At first Clark was happy that Leslie wanted to share his life. He paid more attention to her and went less often to see his other girl-friends. He and Leslie went to museums or to the theater together, played chess and, when they came back home from an evening out, drank a lot of wine and made love. Clark had one of his very few positive dreams after Leslie suggested that they stop drinking for a week. Although it was hard for Clark, he kept his promise and Leslie was very happy. Clark's dream:

> We're in a cheap motel watching TV. To our surprise my younger brother, Philip, appears on TV and sings beautifully. He's the special attraction. I'm astonished and very happy that he has such a beautiful voice and that he has become so successful on television without my help.
>
> Then Rita appears. I haven't told her yet that it's over between us and that I'm married to Leslie. Although it's very unpleasant, I hope that I have the strength to tell her the truth. Rita is no longer attractive; she's gained weight and looks rather slovenly. Rita says that she's let herself go because I've spent so little time with her and it didn't seem important any more to take care of herself. She would often get drunk now.
>
> Then I'm with Leslie in our apartment. I go into the bathroom and pee in the indoor pool. I wonder why I'm doing this and decide to use the toilet from now on. I go back to Leslie and ask her, "Why don't we ever use our pool? Why don't we tell our friends that we even have one?" Then I think it over—perhaps they would be envious. Leslie and I are happy to have such a beautiful thing. I feel rich and fulfilled.

The dream reflected the possibility of a new beginning through contrast: Phil, Clark's younger brother, really was the complete opposite of Clark. Phil was simple, honest and had settled on one girl whom he'd met when he was seventeen and to whom he'd remained true ever since. He was in medical school and wasn't drawn to or influenced by Clark's world in any way. Clark often tried to make fun of Philip, but secretly he envied him.

On the subjective level one could say that a positive side of Clark had emerged in the alcohol-free week during which his connection with Leslie was so harmonious. He hadn't experienced this in a long time and it reminded him of Philip. Rita embodied his anima, his feeling side that confronted him in the dream with how he had let himself go. The drinking was a symbol of his lack of consciousness when he didn't take care of himself.

Clark described Rita as a very nice but weak and superficial woman who didn't criticize him or make any demands on him. She loved going to fancy places and he had spent many enjoyable evenings in her company. The dream showed him that he had almost come far enough to be able to give up this pleasure seeking. In addition, it showed him what fulfillment would be granted him if he replaced the Rita-anima with the Leslie-anima.

The discovery that his inner being (his house in the dream) had a small pool was the discovery of the last week, in which he had won through to a small piece of authentic life. As is frequently the case, he associated water to the beginning of life, to one of the four elements, good and refreshing, to nearness to nature, to the source of our being. Now, granted, there is a big difference whether someone dreams of a spring of water in nature or of an indoor pool in an apartment. Still, it represents a higher value than the bars and nightclubs that had previously figured most often in his dreams.

We all thought that Clark's dream and his conscious sense of well-being with Leslie in their more normal way of life in the last week would lead to a turning point in his life and in their marriage. Leslie was very optimistic. Clark had no doubt that sobriety would be their new lifestyle from now on and he anticipated being in a better condition to overcome his writer's block. However, after a few days these good intentions came to naught. After a bad day at the office where one of the directors had criticized his show as superficial and empty, Clark went out to eat with a few friends and got thoroughly drunk.

Although Clark began to drink again, Leslie kept to her resolution not to touch alcohol. She took pains to get Clark to stop and was constantly afraid of losing him. Since she was no longer prepared to share his drinking, he suggested that she give up her "prudery" and try three-way sex with him. Hesitating and more afraid than shocked, she agreed. She had the following dream after a series of such encounters:

I'm dancing in the middle of the street at Times Square. It's dark. I'm dancing in a tiny, black lace bikini. Trucks and cars are driving all around me and the drivers make remarks. I offer myself to them all with open gestures.

John: "How did you feel when you woke up?"

Leslie: "Sexy and in a bad mood—both."

Hanna: "No wonder—you're really living an awful life—where's it going to end?"

Eric: "And it's so dark in the dream, you're in danger of being run over in the middle of the road."

Leslie: "Yes, I felt like I was in danger."

Clark: "Nobody dies from sex."

Eric: "That's not the point! As if you didn't know it!"

Renée: "Clark, what do you think the dream is referring to? What is it saying to Leslie? What is it saying to you?"

Clark: "We were together with another woman. It was terrific. It's all new to Leslie, but she's very good. When the woman left we had a fight. I went out to get a drink. I thought that in between she would cook something ahead for the next day. Then we fought again because I'd had a few. She wanted to sleep in the living room. I said, 'No, I'll sleep in there.' Back and forth—it's all so boring."

Leslie: "Not for me—I will not live this way anymore. All I dream about is sex. That's all we talk about. I wanted to go to college. Now it's like the dream—nothing is private. I feel like a whore, really, as though I'm selling myself on Time's Square. All those cars . . ."

Hilda: "I see the cars as a means that other people use to accomplish their goals. One person is driving to college, another goes from his business to his home, and another drives to work. They're all your average, normal citizens. But what stands for security for others is a danger for her."

Leslie: "But I must have something of this whore side in me, otherwise I wouldn't dream about it."

Renée: "What is most critical, it seems to me, is that you would like to bring together the two sides of yourself, but you're not ready.

The provocative outfit and wanting to seduce the men are on the one side and the normal, everyday atmosphere of Time's Square is on the other. Many of us have different sides—more than just two such opposites—but to live as you are, you will surely be run over."

Leslie: "Last night I thought that if this goes on much longer, I'll have a nervous breakdown!"

Clark: "But you said yourself that you've enjoyed these games we play with the other women."

Leslie: "Yes, that's true and it's not true. Yesterday we visited the two lesbians and watched them make love. It was exciting, but afterwards I had such a frightening dream. We have this splendid sex circus going on and afterward I always have the feeling that there's absolutely nothing between us."

Martin: "It seems that only your quarreling is private."

Leslie: "I feel that I'm taking up too much of the group's time."

Eric: "I wanted to tell one of my dreams, but I have the feeling that you need this more. Go ahead and tell your other dream. Maybe it'll help. I can wait until the next time."

Renée: "I think there's hardly a woman who hasn't had fantasies about homosexuality, sadism, masochism, promiscuity or prostitution. But such things are seldom spoken of in company. Maybe it would help us all to talk about it openly in the group."

Hilda: "That would really help. If you talk about it, maybe I'll be able to talk about myself and my fantasies the next time."

Leslie: "I'm really grateful to you. I'm so mixed up that I don't even know right from wrong anymore. I think the next dream has something to do with that. But I can't see it. With my Time's Square dream I can begin to get something—my whorish side—I must learn to understand it rather than just condemn it."

John: "As long as you suppress it with guilt feelings and shame, you'll never be done with it."

Leslie: "I understand this everyday side, the conventional side, better than the other, but I have to be free of it too, or at least change it. Okay, now for the dream:

I'm looking at photos of naked women; they're very sexy. My mother is there and I want her to look at them too. Somehow I have a feeling of danger, but I'm not sure why. Then there are long corridors like in a convent school. Women in long black habits with white collars wander continuously through the house. I must kill them all. I have a sharp ax. I don't know if the women are nuns or whores, but I attack each one that I see. The ax is heavy and carries out its work well. I strike one exactly between her breasts and split the skull of another in two. If one isn't completely dead, I keep striking until she is. I'm acting as if under compulsion. I have to kill them all out of self-defense. Wherever I go, there's blood everywhere.

Tom: "That's gruesome!"

Martin: "What was going on with you two? Another fight?"

Clark (ironically to Leslie): "Did Clark get drunk again and go after you with an ax?"

John (turning to Clark): "Would you like to tell us what really happened? Leslie seems to be very unhappy." (Leslie is crying.)

Clark: "We were in a really good mood when we came back home after seeing the two lesbians. We cooked dinner together and talked about Leslie's childhood, the early teenage years, and about how strict the nuns were in the convent school. I said they'd never be able to help her become a real woman. This whole convent school—you've got to eradicate it root and branch!"

Leslie: "Yes, but I said that I'd also gotten to know about many good and beautiful things from the nuns. Clark just stuck to his view that I had to throw my whole past overboard. I wasn't clear about whether he was right or whether I could even do it. How do you throw your past overboard?"

Hanna: "How did the evening end?"

Leslie: "Clark went to bed. I just wanted to look over a recipe and suddenly, without thinking about it, I called my mother up and told her I wanted to come for a visit. She was so happy. I told her I'd come in a few days. As I hung up the phone, I was very happy, but I cried terribly afterward. Then I went to bed."

Hilda: "If you understand 'eradicate' to mean that you have to take an ax to everything having to do with the nuns, then it's no wonder you're so confused."

Clark: "I'm sorry—I didn't know that struck you like that. I didn't want that to happen!"

Leslie: "I know. I'm not angry with you. I'm just not myself. So much sex—so much brutality—that's why I think I will go home. I have to orient myself differently, go somewhere where everything is more simple."

Renée: "I think that's a good idea. Maybe everything will be a little clearer then."

Eric: "It could also be a little rocky. Your mother, the life there, your family—it might strike you as very bourgeois."

Leslie: "I know, but that doesn't frighten me—that's what I want. I have to go back once more to where I came from—to look at everything once more, the old world and the new world in which I live now. But I have to be free of Clark's influence to do it."

Clark: "I think Leslie is right. I envy her! I wish I could get some release from my confusion by visiting my parents."

Leslie went home and Clark had good reason to envy her. His dreams were an endless chain of women whom he seduced, of men who were having nervous breakdowns, and of work that was being ignored. After Leslie's departure, naturally the first thing that took place was a small orgy. Clark was, as always, very satisfied with himself, showing off his masculinity and being unbearably conceited. His unconscious reacted in a typical way to his behavior. His next dream went as follows:

> Doris and I are in the pool. She is naked. I take off my clothes too and become aware that my testicles are big and very heavy. I wonder if she's admiring them. Then suddenly her dogs come running along and sniff at me as if they were getting to know me again. I'm proud of that and say something about it. When I start to go into the water I see that suddenly there are piles of dog shit—all soft and disgusting. There are puddles of dog piss everywhere. I'm horrified and completely confused. I don't know

what to do. My clothes are completely soiled as well. Wherever I look, everything is a chaotic and filthy mess.

Clark, who used women for his convenience and to gain admiration, also used his own feeling side to flatter himself. The dogs symbolized—as in Eric's dream—the instinctual side of his nature, which was not very well differentiated. The dog excrement stood for the negative results of his attitude. Clark's dreams were speaking in an ever-clearer language of how his erotic adventures, with no obligation to anything, were defiling everything in and around him. However, he continued to deny that the anxiety and feelings in his dreams had anything to do with his waking life. The more drastic the messages from the unconscious became, the more he drank, while denying even that. He distanced himself increasingly from the group and found that the others would do nothing but reproach him and morally condemn him. In such a crisis an individual session should be fitted in. This took place, but Clark was unreachable.

It was interesting how the dreams of the two gradually, but very clearly, went in different directions and were instrumental in the decisions that Leslie and Clark would reach in the final phase of their counseling. Leslie sent the group a dream from her mother's home where she had decided to extend her stay. She sent the dream without interpretation and only said that she would like to be present when the group considered it so that she could explain how things stood with her and why she had stayed away longer than planned. Here is her dream:

I have built a beautiful castle in the air. People come and want to destroy it, which they start to do. I try to stop them. I try desperately to save it, but it looks as though I won't succeed. It's as if I would be destroyed. If they succeed in destroying my castle, I will disappear into thin air. I start sobbing and implore them, "Please don't destroy my beautiful castle! I beg you!"

She wrote that she woke up then, but not completely, and thought that Clark was lying next to her. Still crying she said to him, "Clark, don't wreck my castle. Please don't destroy my beautiful castle!" She closed the letter with the words: "Comments are superfluous. I miss you all terribly!"

When the letter had been read, only Martin had something to say. "She only thinks she would disappear into thin air if the house of cards fell down. She has to give up the illusions she has about Clark. Only then would the marriage have a real chance. I wouldn't want to be prince of a castle in the air either!"

We were not all of the same opinion, but one thing was sure: Leslie could not continue to live in a castle in the air which was painted with the colors of love and passion and perhaps with the blood from her last dream. She has to finally come back to reality. It would seem that the visit to her mother and some distance from her life with Clark was helping her to see things more clearly. It was understandable that she feared a nervous collapse, if all of her hopes, wishes and plans for her life with Clark were to break apart and prove to be an illusion.

Clark, who was present at this session, said that he had had a dream after receiving a letter from Leslie. For the first time, he seemed to have considered for a moment the possibility that Leslie could leave him. He looked worn out and nervous. Here is his dream:

I'm sitting with two psychiatrists in white coats in the cafeteria of a hospital; it seems to be a mental institution. They're talking with John about their theories of analyzing a resistance. They're laughing and are friendly, but they're making fun of John. I feel that I should come to his defense. I would like to say that it would do me good if I could give up my resistance . . . but I don't say anything. I feel flattered that the psychiatrists have included me in their conversation and I don't want to put that at risk while taking John's part.

Then I meet Gail. I admire her beautiful hair and ask myself whether I should start something with her. I feel that I should—that she expects it. We go into the house and I try to kiss her. She resists but I think she's only playing. She turns away and I notice that something is wrong with the house. The hall is full of garbage. The walls have big cracks. The whole building is on the verge of collapse.

I wake up frightened.

John: "Am I the 'John' in your dream?"

Clark: "I hope you're not offended."

John: "It's your dream—your inner psychologist. It is you who have developed resistance to the therapy and I'll bet you have also developed a whole theory to explain it."

Clark: "Yeah, that's true. What can I say? I laugh at myself and my resistance. I've also thought that maybe I should go to a psychiatrist rather than a psychologist."

Martin: "Go ahead and try. I went to a psychiatrist and he didn't help me nearly as much as our group here with John and Renée."

Eric (to Clark): "It's just your snobbishness talking."

Hilda: "That dream is frightening . . . the crumbling wall . . . your house caving in . . . that says it all: your marriage, your life, yourself!"

Hanna: " . . . and at the same time that Leslie's house or castle in the air is collapsing."

Clark said that he'd like to save his marriage, but didn't know how. It was hard to advise him because he was still not ready to change his lifestyle or his outlook on life. I was sorry about him; he was talented and had a lot of good qualities behind that conceited façade. The insatiable hunger for ego-boosts could have found an answer in an authentic masculinity and in real achievement. In spite of all his success in television, real accomplishment meant only one thing for him: writing his novel. It upset him that he couldn't bring discipline to the writing and instead pursued women and alcohol. Leslie was different. She earnestly took pains to grow and to become a stronger, more self-reliant person.

It was much easier for her to say "no" to sensuous pleasures. She could also easily give up drinking. She had no problem sticking to a diet or completing a given assignment on time. She had the necessary prerequisites for a happy and fulfilling life. She could have helped Clark too, but he was too proud to let himself be helped by "such a child."

When Leslie returned she had changed—more serious, no longer "the sweet young thing." She seemed stronger and more grown up. She came alone to therapy; Clark didn't feel well.

"Is he drinking?" asked Tom.

Leslie nodded, but it didn't seem to concern her. She told the group that she was leaning toward a divorce and had definitely decided on a separation. She had registered at a college and wanted to study psychology. It was no longer important, or so she said anyway, whether Clark approved or not. That sounded a little too sure. It didn't seem believable that she had gotten free of Clark in such a short time. I made a remark to that effect, but she thought otherwise. She said she had had a dream that would show me how free she was:

I'm in college—in Experimental Psychology. A young man is mentally disturbed. To my surprise, Michael, an actor whom I know, is my teacher. I tell him that the young man needs help. He says I should help him. I'm nervous and feel unsure of myself. Can I help him? Do I even know what's going on with him?

Then I'm with Michael in his apartment. I'm delighted that he's going to be my teacher. He's sitting calmly in his chair; he's unbelievably handsome. I realize now that I've always longed for him. I'm drawn to him and fascinated by him. I think to myself, "I must have this man." He seems to be mad at me and leaves. I run after him. My feeling for him is very strong.

Then I'm near a house that is haunted. A woman goes into the house. Her husband, from whom she has been separated for a long time, has lived there alone for many years. Everyone has warned her not to go back. Why does she do it? I don't know. It's very creepy.

Martin: "Do you really believe the dream shows how free you are?"

Eric: "You sound abrasive and sarcastic, Martin—what's going on?"

Martin: "At the end she goes back into the haunted house—that's her marriage she's going back to!"

Hanna: "You can't judge a wife just because she hesitates. It would almost be abnormal if she didn't."

Hilda (to Leslie): "And, look, you already have a new 'glamour boy' in your dream. You're no different than your husband . . ."

Renée (intervening as Leslie looked more and more confused and frightened): "I wonder why you all are so miffed at Leslie."

Hilda: "I don't understand why you're not also mad. She's not even free from Clark yet and here she is grabbing hold of a new man—this 'Michael' whom she's talked about for a long time. Just another television actor, a younger version of Clark."

Leslie: "He's not just any old actor; he's very serious about his work."

Renée: "I don't think that's what it's all about. That doesn't seem important to me."

Eric: "What is important? I can only say I'm disappointed."

Martin: "Yeah, that's it. I thought the same thing, but I didn't want to say it. I felt that I didn't have a right to be disappointed with Leslie."

John: "You've all put yourselves up on a pedestal. Do you know why you're so disappointed?"

Hanna: "I'm not at all disappointed. I think it's good. After all the dream shows that she's enrolled in college."

Leslie: "Yes, I thought that too, but now I'm not finding the dream so good. 'Experimental Psychology'—that sounds like I wanted to experiment around with psychology and with the psychology professor. I've already had every possible fantasy about meeting a young professor who falls in love with me—I'll become the professor's wife—and then of course he should also be handsome and actually like an actor who plays the role of a professor. How I run after him in the dream! I don't like that at all anymore."

Martin: "So Michael is not an ideal animus figure. Something isn't right there—I don't know—even disappointing; understandable but disappointing."

Renée: "With Clark, Leslie was the wife of a well-known producer. Next she's the wife of a young professor. I don't think you can find your life and identity through men; sooner or later you must find them in yourself."

Hilda: "That's it—that's what made me so angry. Now I understand it. I wanted Leslie to be strong."

Eric: "Yes, that was also my ideal. You separate from Clark, are immediately strong and self-sufficient, find yourself a serious male student and you study together, and so on and so on."

Leslie: "I hardly understand what it means to find my own identity, to stand on my own two feet and accept my own qualities—all that. How do you do that? How do you get there?"

Hanna: "I don't know yet either, but I have an idea. For a long time I wanted my husband to get ahead in his career so that I would have more status. Now I've started to develop my own talents and I don't pressure him anymore about his work. That's his business."

Leslie: "Yes, I understand now what you all mean about the secretary marrying the boss. I thought that I had it made—but what does that mean? I'm asking myself that for the first time. And I also don't know what all the sex is about."

Renée: "Judging from your dream, the sexual aspect is not the real problem. That you always have to lean on a man—that's the problem. That is the mentally disturbed young man in the dream—an animus dependent on help from his surroundings. When you are feeling distraught, you flee into your wifely role. You use sex (the black bikini) to catch a man who then is supposed to boost you with his name and accomplishments so that you don't need to accomplish things yourself."

Hanna: "It took me a long time to have confidence in myself."

Leslie: "Yes, I have the feeling that I'm completely empty—worthless—I'm just a big nothing!"

John: "A nothing—the helpless young animus figure said, 'I need help,' but your dream says that you should help him."

Leslie: "Do you know what I can do? I have to do something to become stronger, to achieve some worth myself. Then I'll stop feeling that I'm nothing."

John: "Whatever you do, you shouldn't go back into your haunted house. Do you see the connection between the man, whom you 'hunger' after, whom you 'must have,' who should be your salvation, and the dependence of the woman in the next section of the dream?"

Leslie: "The scary house, the wife who keeps going back."

John: "Yes, the dream is saying that the woman will never be free—she keeps looking for a man to save her, even when everything is old and eerie like the house in the dream."

Leslie nodded: "It seems so hard not to lean on someone."

Renée: "It's easier to carry the true burden oneself than it is to carry the false one."

Hanna: "I think that goes for us all—definitely for me."

The true burden and the false one remained the theme for the rest of the evening. That had also been the problem for Tom and Elli. The shadow of her dead mother, whose morality stood between the young couple, was the false burden for Elli. The true burden was to take on the responsibility for her sexual wishes herself. Also it was easy for Eric to recognize that his false burden was the guilt feelings over his homosexual escapades. They disappeared when he took it upon himself to look for and to strengthen his masculine identity at work and in his marriage.

Following the group discussion, John and I continued to talk about our views concerning the problem of continuing or dissolving a marriage. John, as a young psychologist and a beginning marriage counselor, admitted how hard it was for him to resist taking sides—for Leslie against Clark, for Hanna against Eric. Only with Tom and Elli had he succeeded in keeping free of any opinion. I wanted to know why this was so. He told me that, since they were both so young, he felt that he had helped them almost as a teacher would have. Also, he was not identified with either of them. That was the salient point!

John said he was happy that Leslie had learned the meaning of the dreams, which could serve as support in bringing to bear her own feelings and moral values. "But I still don't know exactly what I should think about the whole thing," he said. "One has to consider that Leslie has much that is good from Clark and that he could make something positive of the marriage if he wanted to."

"If he wanted to," I replied, "but up to now he hasn't wanted to."

"Doesn't that make you angry?" John wanted to know.

"No," I said, "I've learned to be more interested in the dreams and the suggestions they give, than in what an individual does with them."

John: "Sometimes I'm very sorry that Clark doesn't see at all how beautiful and fulfilling his life could be."

Renée: "Yes, I feel that too sometimes, but I know that the therapy goes awry when it's more important to me than it is to him that he live a fulfilling life. I feel sorry, but I keep a certain distance from that feeling so that a spark doesn't fly over from being sorry to active intervention."

John: "I know that, but sometimes I just can't help myself. I want to help, to give advice. I've tried to develop ideas for Clark that could motivate him to work on his novel every day or to drink less."

Renée: "That won't hurt—it's just that it doesn't help. He already knows all that himself."

John: "For me it's tough. I get angry with him when he doesn't follow my advice. What I'd really like to do is punish him."

Renée: "Exactly—just like his parents, his teacher, his wife. This is yet another example of the true and the false burden."

John: "That's good. I'm going to reflect on that. That Clark hears the suggestions given in his dreams, that I help make them understandable and then leave it all to him—that is the light burden. But if I insist that he follow my advice and do everything 'right' and then get angry if he doesn't, *that* is the heavy burden."

Renée: "Yes, and on top of that is the fact that you can't force him to do what you think is right anyway."

To adopt a "wait and see" attitude was the most difficult thing for John to do when the problem was separation and divorce with all the emotional ups and downs and contradictory decisions involved.

When one of the partners decides to divorce, a feeling of euphoria usually follows. The other partner, who can't yet accept a separation, often falls into a depression or thinks of ways to get even. Yet neither the euphoria nor the depression is genuine. One person says how splendid life will be from now on; the other says how frightening and hopeless everything is.

Family and friends often make the mistake of wanting to intervene and appease and to list all the things the partners have in common. But it doesn't depend on that. The good things don't need a testimonial. It's the difficulties that must be attended to. One can't make it clear enough to the couple that the shared life has its price just as much as the single life. Living together means relinquishing a certain amount of freedom. In addition, one lives with the criticism of the partner whose personal limitations one must accept.

The price of living alone consists of other difficulties, which can lead to feelings of painful loneliness, especially during holidays and vacations. In our society there are so many occasions when the single person feels like a fifth wheel. One has to know oneself well in order to know what price one can pay.

One of the most important tasks of the couple counselor is to discuss these questions thoroughly, especially when the client (like Leslie) is convinced that he or she understands the situation. In Leslie's case, particularly, the single life was not without danger, since she was so quick to attach herself to a man and to expect guidance and meaning to come from him. At the moment she had no idea how lonely she could feel and how strong the temptation would be to either run back to Clark or slip into another similar relationship—with Michael, for example.

We thought about what circumstances and what type of woman it would take for things to go well in a marriage with Clark. John thought that it ought to be a woman who was not too young, one who had already had her own experiences. We both agreed that, above all, Clark needed a woman who would enjoy his lifestyle, a woman who wouldn't want to change him and who would not have conflicts of conscience over their way of life. Joy, his friend for many years, would have been far more suitable for him than Leslie. Playing around in threesomes wasn't a problem for Joy because sex and feeling were two completely separate things for her.

John admitted that at first he was shocked at Clark's love life.

"Now I don't think that's so important," I said. "What seems important to me is that the participants are not hurt. When everyone agrees on what they want, what they enjoy, it's not up to the counselor to say, 'My wife and I would never do that!' "

John laughed, "Yeah, that's about what I'd like to have said, but then, for the first time, I thought about my prejudice and the group's, and I came to a similar conclusion."

"That also goes for the sadomasochistic, erotic games of partners, which are so often condemned by the group; but so long as they enjoy them . . .? It is something else if one of them suffers, or—as in Leslie's case—only takes part in something that is false for her in order not to lose her partner."

John said, "That is actually the way it is in every marriage; it's not so much about right and wrong. Even with Eric, what was important was that he wanted to be free of his homosexual behavior and suffered when he couldn't reach that goal."

Then we talked about just how often the marital war is fought out on the plane of right and wrong and how the counselor must be very careful to avoid being pulled in by one's own wishes and limitations.

John said that his marriage was a good example in this regard. "I'm the kind of man who doesn't like to help in the kitchen. When I talked about this in the group during my own therapy, all of the women there were upset by my position. They took me for an enemy of women, one of those who think that women belong in the kitchen. Oh yes, they knew all about it!

"Then I met Mara, my present wife. When she invited me over for dinner the first time and I offered to help with the dishes, she said, 'Thanks, but the kitchen is my domain. I don't like to share it with anyone, least of all a man.' The group thought Mara was completely old-fashioned and dependent on men. No discussion could take place. The group leader always took sides; right and wrong were argued over constantly, with the therapist taking the position of chief judge."

"It's good that you were with him," I said, "Because at least you learned what one should not do!"

John said, "Yes, whenever I'm tempted to play the authority figure, I think about that fellow and then I know right away that that won't do. Sometimes it's really difficult."

I could only agree with him, and added that a genuine interest in the people in the group and a certain distance from them were not incompatible. "The less you are personally engaged in wanting a situation to be resolved in this or that way, the better you hear what is really going on with the couple. Stay as close to the dream as you can, then you'll never lose your sense of security."

John had an opportunity to prove this insight during a session when Clark told a dream that gave rise to much dissension in the group.

> We are together with William Faulkner and his friend, Liam. We—by that I always mean Leslie—but I notice that she's not there. Liam is a forty-five-year-old, self-destructive man. We're getting ready to leave and are packing and sorting things. We're waiting for Joy. I'm worried because Leslie isn't there. Finally she appears. I see her coming down the stairs with those small hurried steps that I love so much. My heart thumps for a moment and I'm happy she's there. We all leave the island and get on a boat. The boat drives over dry land for a while before it comes to the water. Faulkner and Liam are drinking heavily during the trip and are having endless and boring discussions about examples of infidelity.

Clark continued, "Then I had a second dream":

> I'm the King of France. I'm inspecting the palace and decide that I will have four queens and a special throne room for each of them. As I go through the palace, people treat me with indifference. I'm not against democratic behavior, but I'm afraid that I have no power. I demand to see the Chief of Protocol so that I can settle how I should be treated. I wake up before he arrives. I'm afraid that I've lost my power and I don't know what I can do to regain it.

Martin jumped at the dream right away: "Just as detestable as all your dreams—women, women . . ."

Leslie: "Why does Clark's fun with sex disturb you so? As though he had no other priorities and did nothing else with his life but drink and go to bed with women. Why is that always so important to you? I think you're just a dumb middle-class jerk."

Hanna: "I think it's great that you can say that." Turning to Clark, "I don't like how you live, Clark, but I no longer find it so damnable."

Eric: "Too bad, it looks like we've lost our scapegoat."

Clark (very quietly): "I do what I can to keep Leslie. I don't want to hurt her; I love her."

Leslie (crying): "I know that."

Hilda: "I'm furious with you, Clark, not because your marriage isn't working, but because you know so much about yourself, you've had years of therapy, and yet you make so little effort to change."

Clark: "I believe I'm weaker than you think. I don't mean this as an excuse. The dream is painful to me. My good 'we,' my Leslie, is no longer there. What will I do without you?"

Leslie cried harder and laid her head on Clark's shoulder. He had tears in his eyes too. Everyone in the group felt the pain of these two people who had strong feelings for each other, and yet no longer seemed to be able to find a way to stay together. No one felt like pursuing Clark any longer or saying disagreeable things to him. Leslie spoke first.

Leslie: "Clark has so many good qualities. Even here in the group he never gets caught up in these little disputes. He doesn't talk about people behind their backs—and he is so good to his friends."

John: "By chance I know one of your friends, who told me enthusiastically how nice you are to your colleagues, Clark, how you help people get ahead in their careers, how generous you are . . ."

Leslie: "Yes, and not only with money! He helps them get honor and recognition that he's actually entitled to."

Clark: "Stop! That's nothing! Those things are easy for me. But the drinking—that is getting worse and worse and it depresses me, which is a reason to drink more. Then, naturally, I don't write anything that's any good."

Hanna: "Do you mean the novel?"

Eric: "Have you talked to Renée? Are you in individual therapy?"

Clark: "Yes, she says that my drinking is not a psychological problem, but a spiritual one. At first I laughed at that, but now I know that, unfortunately, it's true. But I doubt whether I have the spiritual strength to muster an inner sense of responsibility for myself."

John: "If you don't do it, you'll destroy yourself."

Clark: "I know."

Martin took over at this point. We continued to discuss the theme of self-destruction. Finally Clark, who had been quiet for a long time, said, "I don't think I want to come here anymore. Maybe I'll go into individual therapy, perhaps with Renée, perhaps not. I've spent six years with various analysts. What I would need now is Alcoholics Anonymous, but I just can't bring myself to do that yet. I want to do this alone. Up to now I've thought more highly of myself than I do of the people who go to those meetings."

Renée: "The hardest thing for an alcoholic is to admit that drinking is a problem that he can't solve by himself."

Clark: "I'll come once more next week in any case. I want to see what my dreams say about my decision."

Martin: "I hope you'll stay with us. If you really get a divorce, you're going to need us. We're better friends than a whiskey bottle."

Following the session John told me how much more free he felt after the group's discussion. He looked at the dream—the desert-like land through which the boat must go before reaching the water, the element of life. Instead of taking sides, he saw how both partners were helplessly caught in their problems.

Clark, with his wish to be king, had forfeited his power. Basically the problem had more to do with inflation than with power. His hope to save the little prestige that he still had as king with the help of his "Chief of Protocol" was pathetic. John interpreted this as Clark's hope to preserve at least a façade so that his friends and colleagues wouldn't learn how things really stood with him and his marriage— that he was basically powerless in relation to everything that was important to him.

"I saw suddenly how hollow, how exhausted, Clark is," said John. "He's close to a nervous breakdown."

I too had the feeling he couldn't go on like this much longer, but that he knew, too, that probably no one could stop him. At least neither the group nor I was able to. Maybe he wanted to have a breakdown and go to the hospital. Maybe that seemed easier than going to meetings of Alcoholics Anonymous. He would be able to admit that he was sick, but not that he was weak.

The separation was hard on Clark and Leslie. Again and again they went from quarreling to reconciliation and sexual intimacy. The dreams that followed the quickly shifting arguments and short-lived reconciliations became more and more gloomy. Meanwhile Leslie was completely wrapped up in her college courses. She was very attracted to one of the students of her own age, but took to heart the group's warning about not falling head over heels in love. Clark drank and cut himself off from society. They missed some therapy sessions because their arguments usually took place in those evening hours when the group met.

When they turned up in the group again, both of them wanted to discuss the dreams they had had on the same night. (Following a violent argument that had come to blows, Clark had stayed in the apartment while Leslie had gone to a friend's house to spend the night.)

Clark's dream:

I propose a film to the directors that seems to me to have enormous meaning. It's about a man whose stomach is opened. His intestines fall out and he holds them in his hand and studies them. The attitude of the man to what has happened is of the utmost importance for the film. The man takes the situation completely naturally and feels at the same time that a once-in-a-lifetime opportunity has been given him to study his insides.

As he lies there examining them, he says, "That's me—Clark, how amazing!" He does so in the certainty that this one-time opportunity comes with a high price. The man will undoubtedly die from the consequences. In order to represent the man in the right way, it is crucial to know that he accepts his death and wants to spend his final moments studying his insides. One of the directors asks, "Does he have any pain?" "No," I say, " he's in a state of shock, so that he can't feel any pain."

The dream was so expressive that one didn't need to ask how things had gone the night before. The mortal fear that Clark felt at the idea of studying his inner being, and the symbolism of group therapy as a surgical procedure that would let him bleed to death, made it not only understandable but urgent that he give up this kind of therapy at this time. Therefore we weren't surprised when he told us that this would be his last session.

Hanna: "What are you feeling?"

Clark: "Last night when Leslie left I sat at the table alone. I felt washed out. I've gained so much weight. I have an insatiable craving for alcohol and sensual pleasure and I'm completely overwhelmed by the pathetic nature of my work. 'Nothing good comes from this man!' "

Leslie (in a gentle voice): "I think you should go to a hospital. First you need to have the alcohol washed out of your body. Then all of the other decisions will be easier."

Clark: "Tomorrow I'm seeing someone who is a doctor and psychiatrist. He's dealt with many alcoholics."

Hanna: "Leslie, what happened last night in your dream? You look so pale and unhappy."

Leslie: "It was horrible"—

We're in our apartment. Clark wants to kill me. He poisons the wine. I see him do it, but I can't do anything about it. I'm completely passive. I drink the wine and fall down almost unconscious on the couch. Clark watches me in a cool manner. I think to myself that if dying is this easy, I don't have anything against it. But then I wake up—in the dream—and realize that I'm not dead yet. Now I'm terribly angry. Clark is furious that it hasn't worked and tries to smother me with a kiss. That doesn't work either. Although I think again that I'm dead, I'm still alive.

Now he tries to break my nose with his fingers. He tears it off my face and says, "Now you are separated from your nerve center and you will either die or bleed to death." My nose has been ripped off. Hot blood is streaming over me. I'm naked and stumble out into the street. My breasts are covered with blood. It must be a dreadful sight. I need help.

I meet my mother. I beg her for help, but she doesn't listen and goes into our apartment house to the elevator. I follow, but she still doesn't listen to me. We get out on our corridor. I go into our apartment. I think she is behind me, but she has disappeared. Clark is there. I'm deathly afraid. He's sitting very calmly in a chair with a knife in his hand waiting for me. I scream, "You can't do this! What do you want?" He says, "I don't know yet."

"I woke up shaking with fear. Afterward I couldn't get the dream out of my mind for hours."

The final stage of their marriage was finished. However, this was definitely not the end of their psychotherapy. Clark, who was on the verge of breaking down, needed the protection of a hospital and then intensive individual therapy in order to be ready to deal with his drinking problem. Leslie needed contact with John and me as well as the help of the group. The delusion that there was still something to be salvaged from her romantic fantasy of marriage needed a stark confrontation with her unconscious. Her dream expressed a warning that was more than clear: "If you continue to allow yourself to be exposed to danger by your weak animus, you will either die outright or bleed to death."

On account of her weakness she believed that Clark was ruined and she felt she was going to die. Her mother, who represented her own maternal nature, even turned away from her in the dream. (Her real mother had actually turned away from her when she spoke to her about a possible divorce.) All of her positive functions were destroyed. Therefore we weren't surprised when she confessed that she had tried to take her life while at her friend's house. She felt her "inner Clark" only reflected the worst sides of the real Clark—his weaknesses and destructive tendencies. The dream held up a mirror to her.

"First," I said, "you would poison yourself with sleeping pills and when that didn't work, you stick your head into a plastic bag. If someone else were to do that to you in reality, you would want to save yourself, run away, seek help. The dream wants to show you what you are doing to yourself."

"I wouldn't do that to my worst enemy," said Leslie, very pale.

"But you do that to yourself," I said.

We all felt there was nothing left to say after that dream. Now it was time to act. Clark and Leslie decided that Leslie should move out the next day and that she would get a part-time job near her school. In addition, she needed and wanted both individual and group therapy. The group, although ostensibly for couples, decided unanimously to keep Leslie until she was no longer a threat to herself. Clark was determined to go to a hospital. Both were incredibly sad. Their house of cards was destroyed, and at the moment they had no way to reach each other. Both were too exhausted to talk about divorce. First it was important that they separate.

In discussing the separation later, John and I felt that it wouldn't take long for Leslie to get to know other students at the college and that she would probably be more mature in her choice of a partner the next time.

At the beginning of this chapter I said that the end of therapy is near when the couple is ready to accept responsibility for their own problems and to work on them together in a constructive way. In Clark's and Leslie's case that failed to happen. The dreams showed that the marriage had become destructive to both of them and had actually dissolved of itself; however, the counseling led to their being able to recognize their difficulties and to help each other, with understanding and respect, do what was right for both of them.

In the above-mentioned case of Herman and Mary, as well, the solution was less than ideal: For a woman in the change of life to have to admit that her husband is mentally ill and would likely remain so is depressing and anything but positive. In this case, the marriage counselor helped Mary to reach a decision that was easier for her when she saw from her husband's dreams how much he needed her. His need for help and support was not destructive to this very maternal woman. On the contrary, she felt this to be a task that she could fulfill.

Sometimes the marriage counselor runs the danger of aiming for specific goals for a couple. Counselors should never set goals; rather they should faithfully follow the direction of the unconscious, as revealed by the dreams. This is particularly important during the final phase of therapy when the decisions to stay in or to leave a marriage are being made. There is no universally valid model or form of marriage, only individual couples who must find different ways. Every solution is only valid for the particular couple that finds it. Therefore all the group's well-meaning advice on questions that begin with such words as: "Isn't it natural that a married person should expect . . .?" is wrong. Nothing is "natural." Everything depends on consent and accord between two people.

Couple counselors have done their job successfully if they have worked, from the beginning, toward the partners' being able to talk to each other openly and directly, to listen to each other, and to accept themselves and each other. Then the counselor can take satisfaction in the final phase of therapy knowing that the couple is able to understand and modify their behavior. A small indication from one of them is often enough to make the other partner aware that once again he or she has accused the other instead of helping or accepting some responsibility for a problem.

In the final phase of therapy, decisions are usually reached as a result of a long process of development. Nevertheless, the finality of the decision often arouses anxiety and the couple will turn to the counselor—as they did in the beginning—with the question, "Do you think this is really the right decision?"

For decades this question has been answered—perhaps following psychoanalysis—with the words: "What would *you* most like to do?" An unobliging therapist of the old school would perhaps say, "I hope that you don't expect me to make the decision for you." Then there is the type of therapist who would gladly play God and say, "In your place I would . . ."

The proper answer to the question, "What should we do?" lies between these extremes. I think the most helpful advice is to take the question to bed and wait for the next dream. With great regularity a dream will provide the answer. It is difficult, however, for the dreamer to discern the answer directly from the dream, since it has just emerged from the unconscious. It is easier for the outside observer, especially a trained therapist, to help make the partners aware of what their own unconscious is saying, nor does the therapist have to play God or hide his or her insight. Rather, the counselor acts as an interpreter, a translator, who helps the couple decipher the message.

Often posing such questions is an expression of insecurity, an indication that the desired end-phase has not yet been reached. When that is the case, the dreams confirm this and show where the partners really stand. Often questions have the intention of moving the problem into the field of vision. The question and the behavior of the person asking differ fundamentally from the beginning of the therapy. In this case, the person asking the question usually has the answer already in the background: "I'm not sure this marriage is right for me, but I don't know how I'm supposed to decide." If the therapist refrains from answering right away, this sentence often follows: "That's not true. I absolutely know this relationship is right for me, but the continuation of the marriage imposes tasks that are difficult for me."

Whether the final phase leads to a renewed relationship or divorce, it is important that the partners understand that marriage, as well as divorce, has a price, and that children and possessions should not become a battleground used for revenge. If the therapy relating to a divorce is successful, the couple does not persist in acrimony; rather, these feelings have been worked through so that the separation can be peaceful.

In the beginning, partners who want to separate but are still bound to each other through feeling or habit may think that the separation will proceed more easily if they have grounds to hate each other. Here it is necessary to explain that hate is as strong a bond as love, whereas indifference and acceptance of one's own responsibilities for the failure of the marriage lead to detachment. The more the couple counselor can remain an interested, but not personally involved, outsider and the less he or she takes the part of one marriage partner over the other, then the easier it will be to help them see where their difficulties lie, what their irreconcilable differences are, how different in personality type they are, and what their dreams have to say.

The last and most important task of the final phase of therapy—provided the partners stay together—is for the couple to have an overview of the road they have traveled before and during therapy; then they can probably go forward with success.

The therapist can warn of obstacles, encourage and help couples plan for the immediate and ongoing future. Many couples remain in loose contact with the counselor, perhaps having formal sessions every month or two. Sometimes it suffices for the counselor to offer to be available for a follow-up appointment if desired. And some couples, who have worked together in a group over a long period and whose therapy has ended, continue to be involved in a support group without a leader.

7
The Case of Mark and Debbie

Until now only portions of counseling have been presented because my purpose has been to show how dreams are used in the different phases of therapy. In this chapter, it will become clear how dreams can fit into the overall counseling of a couple.

A colleague sent Debbie to me at the Country Place.[4] She had just made a half-hearted attempt to commit suicide and he wanted her to spend some time in intensive therapy in a setting away from work and family. She was an editor of a technical magazine, very capable and intelligent, married to a successful engineer. Both were in their late twenties. After seven years of marriage, still childless, they had just decided to adopt a child when their doctor suggested trying an operation that could possibly raise the reproductive ability of the husband.

Debbie was dismayed and upset when Mark refused to undergo the operation. He was afraid and psychotherapy didn't help to overcome his fear. Debbie took Mark's "cowardice," as she called it, badly and that reactivated a series of old marital conflicts that all had to do with his various weaknesses. His refusal to undergo the operation, his unwillingness to share her intellectual interests, his habit of going to bed early after a few hours in front of the TV—these and other problems, both real and imaginary, had led to Debbie's suicide attempt

The couple arrived in a small sleek sports car. I was struck at first glance by how much younger they looked than they really were. She was short and built like a gymnast. He looked like a student with curly hair, lively dark eyes and a somewhat stubborn mouth. One had the impression that one was meeting two people who were dating, not a couple that had been married for seven years. Although she looked

---

[4] [The Country Place was a retreat and treatment center for young people in Litchfield, Connecticut. Renée Nell was its founder and senior therapist.—Ed.]

somewhat pale and weak after two days in the hospital, she basically appeared stronger than he did. He watched her every move in a sensitive way and behaved as if he were a younger, rather shy admirer. If she said something that displeased him, however, he tightened his lips and withdrew into himself.

After a short interview, Debbie went to bed and I had a chance to talk to Mark alone. Right away he took all the blame on himself: he wasn't sensitive enough, he didn't show enough understanding, especially for her desire to have a baby, nor did he take enough interest in her intellectual pursuits.

"Enough—that's enough," I said finally. I observed that perhaps he hadn't really asserted himself enough to earn her respect. He admitted that this was probably the case.

"But," he said, "if I stick to my guns, like now with the operation, you see what happens."

Naturally he felt he was to blame for her suicide attempt. It seemed that she had put him in a position where everything that happened was his fault: "You don't take the trouble to understand me," "You don't spend enough time with me." Those were only a few of her endless accusations. Before he left, I suggested that they begin marriage counseling very soon.

My first hour of therapy with Debbie the next morning strengthened me in that conviction. She complained about his weaknesses, blamed him for not being capable of giving her a baby and, now, for refusing to have the operation. It seemed to me that she didn't want the child so much out of maternal feelings, but rather because she was afraid people might think there was something wrong with her if her husband didn't fit the image of the upper middle-class husband.

Her distribution of the problems in the marriage was very simple: he did everything wrong, she did everything right. Only when I empathized with her, in tones of deepest sympathy, and asked why she didn't leave such an inadequate partner did she begin to name his good qualities. He was good-hearted and easier to get along with than she was. He was intelligent and highly respected at work. She liked to do many things with him; they had fun together. Slowly she admitted that perhaps she had as many problems as he, or even more. Also she was afraid of many things: ice-skating, riding a bike, driving—things Mark liked to do and would have liked to share with her.

I asked if she had tried to help Mark instead of belittling him and loading him down with guilt feelings. Naturally she had done that! She informed me of her attempts in this connection. On Sundays she talked to him for hours about his personal limitations and mistakes and pointed out the connection to earlier experiences in his youth. After three or four hours of amateur analysis, they either ended up fighting or he fell asleep.

"I have to ask myself how he could bring himself to stay awake for four hours," I said.

She had to laugh in spite of herself. Luckily she had a sense of humor, even at her own expense.

"Can you tell me why he has stayed with you for all these years?" I asked Debbie.

She found it interesting that she had never asked herself this question, but thought it was because she was a good cook and had made a beautiful home for them. She had brought interesting people, whom Mark also liked, into their home. She was always full of ideas, many of which she shared with Mark. When she wasn't being neurotic she was fun to be around and he was happy with her.

We talked about her desire for a child and in a frank conversation she recognized that she was not yet mature enough to be a mother. She saw that she must first work on becoming a better wife. At the present time her desire for perfection could have a detrimental effect on a child. She defended herself against this idea. She would never extend her urge for perfection to a child. She had already read all the important books on child rearing. I told her that I preferred the reports of her own dreams to my intuition. I said that then we would not get bogged down in futile discussions. She was in agreement with my method and so we waited for the next dream. It came the following night:

I am in Tino's meat market. It is very full. I look into a glass freezer. There are some very special sweets inside. Everybody in the store is looking at the wonderful treats. I explain to them that this is a very unusual upright freezer. They admire me because I know this. I feel proud and happy and say I have a freezer just like it at home and am in the process of filling it with unusual things.

Then I'm at home. I've just had a baby and I stick it into the glass freezer in the kitchen. It is an unusually beautiful baby girl. I've already given her milk, but I don't know whether she's had enough; besides, I want to give her something special—chocolate milk. Mark says, "No, don't give her that!" I'm furious that he would tell me what to do with my baby. I call up my friend, Helga, and ask her for advice. She says, "If Mark says that you shouldn't do it, then let it go."

Debbie had the following associations to the dream: Tino, the butcher, was a warmhearted Italian, a good family man. The sweets didn't belong in the freezer; there wasn't anything like that really in the store. We talked about Tino as a part of her own personality. He symbolized the simple warmth she possessed. She admitted that accusations and analytical lectures were not a nourishing diet for Mark or her. Sweets were not only candy and the like, but compliments about her work, her house, her husband. She would like to put these trophies in a glass case in order to receive even more admiration.

At this point the dream gives an interesting answer to the question as to why it is so important to her to have a child. The sweets in the butcher's showcase suggest that she wants a baby more as an object of display for which she would receive compliments than from a deeply felt maternal need. The dream work brought many facts as well as fantasies to light. In the first part of the dream everything was so perfect. This tendency continued in the second part: the baby shouldn't just have milk; it had to be chocolate milk.

It was interesting to me that she didn't breastfeed the newborn, but wanted to give her chocolate milk. In her dream Mark represented not only himself, the husband, who wouldn't use the baby as a showpiece to satisfy Debbie's vanity, but also an animus figure for this good quality in herself. She made fun of her need for perfection, but she did place a high value on external appearances. She said too that she could not have become so successful in her profession had she not had a completely rational side.

Helga, Debbie's older friend, who had a very good marriage, often made it clear to her that Mark was right. Debbie could stand Helga's reproofs, even though she was usually sensitive to criticism. Later in Mark's and Debbie's joint counseling, Debbie often said reproachfully, "You make me furious!"—as though he should do something at once to put her in a good mood again. She seemed to be stuck in an adolescent place with this behavior, the demand for perfection and the need to receive compliments.

The dream was a good mirror for Debbie. When her husband came for a visit after ten days, she already had various individual and group therapy sessions behind her. Naturally she had wanted to behave in the same way here at the treatment center as she had with Mark. That, however, didn't go over too well. Here each person was confronted by the other residents and had to give up such behaviors. She made rapid progress and also learned to do some things that she had missed in her adolescence. For example, she learned how to ride a bike from a nineteen-year-old man who was crazy about her. (When one saw them together, Debbie didn't look a day older than he.)

She looked forward to showing Mark her newly discovered cheerful personality. She had warm feelings toward him because she had realized, during hours of therapy, how often she had been unjust to him. However, in the first joint session with Mark, she reverted to her old behavior. John was acting as co-therapist because we assumed that Mark would welcome the support of a man. We were amazed that Debbie showed so little of her newly won capability. After she told Mark that she could ride a bike already and planned to learn to drive, she couldn't refrain from saying that Mark had never had enough patience to teach her anything.

The session had a stormy beginning but after awhile—encouraged by John and me—Mark felt confident enough to begin to criticize

Debbie. They began to communicate with each other more calmly and on a better level than before. She told him about her first dream in order to let him know that she was aware of her own limitations. When she mentioned that she had wanted to give the baby chocolate milk, he interrupted and said, "How remarkable! I had a dream last night about a baby in chocolate-colored water." Then he told it:

> Someone gives me a canning jar with brownish preserving liquid inside. A mummified baby is swimming in the liquid. The doctor and I can't figure out what we should do with the jar and the baby.

We asked Mark about his feelings concerning the adoption, the operation and other things connected with them. He became very tense and spoke hesitatingly about his guilty feelings: what a coward he was, how he had disappointed his wife, and so on. We didn't let him continue like that for long because we wanted to hear what Debbie felt about it. At first she was defensive, but soon her voice cracked; she was close to tears. Mark's idea of a child sounded more convincing and corresponded to a real need. His accompanying fantasies had to do with shared activities. His child didn't have to be perfect or successful; the important thing to him was the emotional relationship. Since Debbie's attempted suicide and her open disappointment in him, he didn't think about adoption anymore. The matter of the baby was mummified for him. He wasn't surprised, therefore, when I said that the adoption of a child didn't appear important at the moment; that it might be better first to address their marital problems and learn how to share activities, as he had hoped to do with a child.

Immediately Debbie's reproaches began again. Although she had also given up thoughts of adoption, she was nonetheless angry that Mark had "embalmed" the matter. As they were leaving the room, she said to Mark in an unfriendly, lecturing tone, "I hope you can see how much work we have to do!"

John and I laughed. I said, "There they go again!" John put his arm around Mark and said to Debbie, "First let's play a game of volleyball; the analysis can come later." After the game both of them were in a wonderful mood. As Mark left to go home, he promised to pay attention to his dreams and to write them down.

The next day he phoned and told us the following:

> I have a garden in which creatures are grown only for their brains. The bodies aren't proportioned right. They stick in the ground with only the throats and heads showing. They're all covered up with veils. I'm observing them.

This dream was obviously meant for his wife. Although John and I tried to make clear to her what she was doing to Mark by constantly disparaging him intellectually, his dream was what made a real impression. Mark often felt that he was deadlocked; in spite of her intelligence, Debbie had done nothing to help him. She had guilt feelings because she didn't seem to be able to relate to his warm feelings; and on top of that she reinforced his already considerable feelings of inferiority. Actually, Mark was also very intelligent and only pretended to be slow, more or less to get even.

The following weeks brought a remarkable change in their way of relating. Mark came regularly on weekends and both of them had more fun together than ever before. Mark was an important player on John's volleyball team and he trusted John completely as a therapist. Mark had a short dream that reflected the transference as well as his own progress:

> I'm lying on the operating table in a hospital. I'm interested in what is going on, but have no pain or fear. I'm actually one of the first people to watch this operation, intended to remove something dead from my body.

On account of the therapy, Mark could recognize that the dead part of himself represented dissatisfaction with his marriage. When he couldn't find a solution, he either became silent or withdrew into sleep. In our therapy sessions Mark became increasingly able to be more assertive. Although Debbie said that she had been waiting for a long time for that, actually she was not happy about it.

Mark's growing independence from Debbie brought new problems. Debbie held fast to the picture of a weak and passive Mark, in whom she couldn't have confidence. At the same time, everyone could see that the change he was going through made her insecure. Then Debbie told us the following dream:

> I'm standing in front of a mirror examining myself. My mother is shouting that I should go somewhere with her. I shout back angrily, "I can't go, I'm going to marry Larry today." Mother says, "No, you're not going to marry him. He called up to say that he doesn't want to marry you." I'm furious and call him up to see if this is true. He tries to wriggle out of it, but finally admits that he doesn't want to marry me. I storm out of the house.

The dream shows her problem to be not as big as she alleged. She doesn't want Mark to develop strength if it means that then things would go contrary to her wishes. The dream and the therapy session following it brought her to tears. In the same night she had another dream, but could only remember the words: *"I'm not able to do it."* She also heard my voice saying, *"It all depends on you!"*

"I'm not able to do it," meant for her that she remained weak and dependent on Mark and had not succeeded in realizing her own strength. She also thought he might leave her.

This session was a turning point in their relationship. She felt weak and wanted help and understanding from Mark. Instead of asking him directly, she started whining and accusing him indirectly. He became more reserved and visibly shut off. She said that life didn't have any meaning and suggested the possibility of suicide. Instead of answering we turned to Mark and asked him how he felt about these repeated threats when things didn't go her way. To our astonishment and Debbie's horror, he said very calmly that he sometimes wished that she were dead so he could be free of her manipulating ways. He added, however, that now that he was feeling stronger, he no longer had such thoughts and believed he could cope with the situation.

The mere fact that Mark could talk this way was a sign of inner growth. Debbie became completely hysterical, started sobbing, and tried in every possible way to get him to take back his words. He remained composed, however, and did not feel guilty. After she had calmed down, we steered the conversation around to the panic she had felt because she was incapable of being alone.

She had tried repeatedly to spend time alone and had found out how restless it made her. Sometimes she went shopping with other residents just so she wouldn't have to be alone. She felt spiritually empty and hopeless about this condition.

Around this time Mark became impatient and wanted Debbie to come home again. She wanted to stay longer at the center. She had undoubtedly learned much in her four-week stay, but she still had a long way to go. Although both of them were afraid they would revert to their old behavior, Mark thought too that they could talk about their mutual behavior patterns and individual limitations. (Doing this didn't lead to arguments and strife anymore, but to laughter, a change in attitude and mutual help.)

We suggested that Debbie go home with Mark and that both come to counseling sessions on the weekend. Debbie was unhappy about Mark's sudden demand, but instead of admitting that she had friends at the center, that she was still dependent on John and me, and that she had shared many activities with the other young people, she attacked Mark by saying, "You're egotistical and inconsiderate! You simply can't stand it that I've led a nice life here without you!"

Mark was quiet and John spoke, "It's hard for me to listen to this stuff from Debbie; how about you?"

"Of course it's hard for me too, but what can I do?" said Mark.

I asked, "What would you like to do?"

"I'd like to drive back to New York and go to the movies; I really don't intend to listen to this the entire evening."

"Well," I said, "why don't you go back to New York?"

Meanwhile Debbie kept shouting at him. She wanted to hear me say that it was too soon for her to leave the treatment center.

Mark said, "I can't shout back when she's like this."

"You could say to her in a friendly way that you don't enjoy listening to these tirades and that you're going back to New York now."

Mark looked at John and then Debbie and back to John with the expression of a swimmer who is about to dive off the ten-meter tower for the first time and is scared out of his wits. Up to now he had crossed his arms and legs. Now he uncrossed his limbs, took a deep breath, looked at John and me once more, and then said softly to Debbie, "I think you better stay here for another week, but I'm not going to spend the weekend here. I don't like what you're doing now and I'm going back to New York." Then he stood up.

It was the first time that he had spoken to her in a friendly and firm way. He left no doubt that he meant what he said.

She broke off her tirade immediately, started crying, and pleaded with him not to leave her. Mark looked at John and me again as though he was waiting for a sign from us, but we sat there with expressionless faces and waited. We knew, as well as he, that this was a decisive moment in their marriage. He summoned all his courage and finally said, "There's no reason to get so upset. I'm not mad at you. I just don't enjoy this kind of weekend. It'll be quiet and pleasant in New York. I'll come up to see you again next week."

Debbie was completely beside herself and said that she'd pack her things in two minutes and would leave with him. He was right; she didn't really need to stay on this week.

At that he broke into loud laughter and said, "This can't be true! It works and it's so simple. I just can't believe it." With that he left the room. She was hysterical and ran after him, hanging onto his arm and begging him to take her with him. He remained friendly and firm and went to his car. As I said goodbye to him he shook his head and smiled. "I still can't believe it's so simple. It's like a miracle. Why didn't anyone ever tell me this secret?"

I reminded him that we had talked at our first meeting about the idea that he could only contribute to a healthy marriage if he reacted in a friendly but strong way. Back then he had answered everything with, "Yes, but . . ." He recalled that now and said, "This is a turning point not only in my marriage but in my life. I'll never again react in such a passive way."

This experience was also a turning point for Debbie. She knew that she could no longer treat Mark like a weak young man to be analyzed and taught every Sunday. Mark's independence showed itself in other ways. His therapist in New York, with whom he had been in treatment for years, had tried continually to dissuade him from taking part in the marriage counseling weekends at the Country Place. Mark was in conflict and had hoped that I would help him with his decision, but I had refused. Afterward Mark had dreamed:

Two Frankenstein monsters are chasing me, but they don't seem too threatening.

He associated his New York therapist and me to the monsters, but he said that these monsters could only frighten small children. After that he had no trouble telling his therapist in New York that he would continue the weekend therapy.

During the next week Debbie dreamed that she was visiting a neighbor, Jean, who was given to hysterics:

Noise was coming from the next room as though men were chasing someone. Jean said, "Don't go in there. They're driving a wild horse out of the house." The horse was invisible. I didn't see it. Then a large balloon with a basket for a gondola floated into the room. Jean said, "We're going soaring—come along with us." I was amazed and frightened, but I climbed into the gondola.

Her association to the woman and the wild horse was hysteria. For her, the balloon flight meant she could trust the elements. Working with the dream gave her hope that perhaps she could give up her hysterical outbursts and entrust herself to the flow of life without being afraid that something awful would happen. At the same time she felt that her husband would straighten things out without everything having to go her way. Going home for her now was like climbing into the gondola of the balloon.

In the weeks at home the old problems did come up, but Debbie and Mark dealt with them differently. When the situation between them became too difficult, they postponed the discussion until the weekend at the Country Place. Meanwhile they planned a vacation trip to Europe. Debbie found it hard to let Mark make the preparations for the trip, but he didn't let her interfere. Instead of quarreling she teased him. As a result they felt like a young couple very much in love.

Debbie's final dream dealt with the theme of adoption that we hadn't touched on again:

> In a marketplace, a typical barker was selling "Familia," a kind of corn-flakes. The product sounded tempting, but I wasn't interested.

This part of the dream was self-explanatory. The idea of a family being sold by a barker in a market!

In the second part of the dream she learned some things from her superior in the nearby office that she didn't know in reality. She felt happy about this new relationship when she suddenly remembered that she had agreed to meet her husband.

The transformation of her superior from the gruff person she really was to a friendly feminine figure and the relaxed job atmosphere showed that she had incorporated her career ambitions into a more relaxed attitude.

In the third part of the dream Debbie was meeting her husband in the doctor's office:

> They were angry because I was late and they hadn't been able to get in touch with her. I laughed and said, "Why are you so upset? I'm only five minutes late." The doctor answered, "With your history of suicide attempts we were concerned. You have to understand that." I had to admit they were right.

When Debbie awoke she felt that her wish to have a child, her domineering attitude toward Mark's operation, and the adolescent attempt at suicide were far behind her. She couldn't believe that so much had taken place in three months. Both Mark and Debbie now felt that a wonderful life lay before them and they wanted to enjoy it fully. When they reported back to us in October after their trip, they assured us that this honeymoon trip was better than the first one.

8
Summary

John and I agree that in couple counseling the relationship itself is the client. In a way we're advising three parties; and we must not forget that, according to Jung's theory, the anima and animus come into play. We now have five different points of view to consider. In addition, the underlying personality type of each partner plays a role. The obvious problems of the couple are usually symptomatic of a deeper underlying psychological disturbance. There are, therefore, a variety of factors to keep in mind.

As long as one approaches the couple's situation from the conscious side, one can only probe the material as a whole quickly; to deal objectively with the situation is more difficult. Although tests are revealing, they demand a great deal of time and are expensive. We are convinced that Jung's dream theory facilitates the dreamer's bringing up questions from the unconscious that arise from the complexity of the situation. Besides, there is another reason to attend to the partners' dreams: irrespective of the experience of the counselor, it is difficult for him or her to remain objective vis-à-vis the couple.

When one works with dreams one receives a truthful representation of the subjective inner situation of the partners. This gives the counselor a secure base from the onset of therapy. For the couple, too, the inclusion of dreams from the standpoint of Jung's understanding creates a research-like atmosphere. That is to say, the dream is like an object of archeological research that is found deep within a person. The dream's meaning must be deciphered.

When they don't have to pay undue attention to the restricting aspects of their symptoms, the partners are able to turn their attention to their individual and common problems. The echo of the unconscious, experienced through the dream, is free of judgment. On this plane there is no right-wrong, good-bad, smart-dumb. Even when

I say to my husband in a dream, "You are really so stupid," this doesn't say anything about my husband. It is my dream. My inner voice is speaking to a part of myself that I describe as stupid. Therefore I have to grapple with my own stupidity instead of my husband's. (It doesn't matter whether or not he really is stupid or I have simply projected that quality onto him.)

Whenever problems are dealt with on this level there is less hostility. The dream opens up to the partners a new objective way of understanding themselves and their problems. Instead of denying that problems exist, dream work often leads to a new common interest, to a bridge to each other. During the weeks or months of consultation one learns to understand the dream material. Many couples continue their shared dream work long after the end of counseling.

Usually it is not advisable to burden the couple with technical terms, but rather to help them find names for the dream symbols. For example, "Brother Ernst is very active again," instead of "My negative animus . . ." Images or pictures are easier to remember than abstract concepts and they are more vital than intellectual theories.

At this point I would like to recall a few of the basic concepts presented here in the first chapter. Although we need to explore the dream on the objective level in order to understand the facts to which it refers, the interpretation on the subjective level is also very productive. With subjective interpretation every person in the dream, as well as the dreamer him- or herself, is an aspect of the personality of the dreamer. Dreams may also reflect the events of the previous day.

The first part of the dream states the theme; the middle, the development; and the message at the end of the dream is directed at restoring the spiritual balance of the dreamer. Dreams have a homeostatic function and want what is best for us, so to speak, while pointing up our weaknesses.

The anima and animus are important considerations in counseling. Recall that the anima is the feminine side of the man, his feeling function; it appears in dreams as a female being. The animus is the masculine side of the woman, her thinking function; it appears as a male figure.

The ego is the center of our consciousness; it is the "I" of the dream. We all have dreams in which we appear younger or older, sick or healthy, or even dying. According to Jung, the ego is the involved, performing function. It puts into action thoughts and wishes, our inner and outer impulses. One can see from dreams whether the ego is strong or weak, whether it is in a condition of inflation or deflation and whether the dreamer identifies with it. The ego is the part of our personality that strives for accomplishment and success.

The persona and the shadow are two psychological aspects of the ego. The persona corresponds to our outward conformity with established norms of behavior. This function is most often dreamt of as clothing. The *shadow*, usually represented by a person of the same gender whom we see in a negative way, represents our unacknowledged aspects.

The Self is the all-encompassing symbol of our conscious and unconscious as a whole. It may be dreamed of as God or a god-like figure as a star, the sun, or some other symbol of a complete-in-itself essence. The Self is the goal toward which the dream strives. It is the symbol of integration, balance and harmony. Integration means to subordinate the achievement- and success-oriented goals of the ego to the service of the higher goals of the Self. Jung called the efforts to do this the process of individuation, and it is a life-long process of individual development and couple counseling.

Five dreams will be cited here to describe five different psychological aspects.

The dream about Aunt Margaret (above, page 10) was chosen to illustrate the analysis of a dream on the objective and subjective levels. Objectively, the aunt reminded the dreamer of an unpleasant, cantankerous relative. She resembled a pushy businesswoman whom he had met the day before. On the subjective level the aunt represented his own contentiousness. The union of the objective and subjective interpretations follows from the fact that the businesswoman's aggression touched off his own aggression.

Bill's dream (page 28) serves as an example of a man's self-destructive relationship to his anima. This negative attitude influenced his entire outlook on life. By projecting it onto his wife he could remain unconscious of much in his life. The immediate goal of dream interpretation was to make him aware of these connections and to give him a task he could work on without fleeing from his real artistic work, which he avoided because he didn't trust his talents.

The third and fourth dreams of a couple (pages 38-39) showed clearly the basic psychological structure of an extraverted woman and an introverted man as well as the difficulties arising from such differences in type. That led to the psychological work by each partner individually and together. The wife's identification with her persona and the husband's fear of contact with other people were the predominant problems.

Another anima dream showed the false conclusions one could come to if one understands Martin's dream of his free spirit who loves nature only on the objective level as a sexual dream (page 66). On the subjective level it was clear that the dreamer had neglected his anima and must do something to establish an inner relationship to her.

His wife's dream (page 68) contained her own shadow side in the figure of a secretive woman snooping around in the attic. In part, the shadow was projected onto the marriage counselor, who should be prevented from guessing the dreamer's secret. The immediate task is indicated right here in the dream—to work through the secret with both partners.

Dreams continually show one or more shadow sides in order to help people to see themselves more clearly. The five aspects named above are contained in almost all dreams. For that reason dreams are important for counseling, apart from their other functions.

In the third chapter we saw how helpful dreams are for diagnosis. Dreams help the counselor understand whether a person is capable of establishing the balance in his or her life for which the dream strives. Here again are the basic points for the diagnosis. The most important consideration for a diagnosis of the dreamer's mental health is to recognize the position of the ego in the dream. How does the ego relate to other people, to things, to events? Actively or passively? In a helpful or destructive manner? Is the dreamer arrogant or subservient?

In the dream of the ruined factory (page 43) we saw a passive man who had no reserves, no strength left. He walked through the factory in which all of the transmission belts had been cut to pieces. A diagnosis of psychosis or of a deep depression was indicated here. Of course one can't make a conclusive diagnosis from one dream, but such a dream should warn the therapist to be cautious until more dreams are related and more is known about the person's medical history.

A further indication of a psychosis can be given through bizarre dream images or situations. Then it is appropriate to ask how the dreamer feels in the situation. If the person is unable to see bizarre aspects of a situation or has no reaction, either in the dream or in reality, then one should explore whether bizarre things actually happen to him in his or her life. As a rule, psychological health is expressed in dreams through appropriate behavior.

In many of the dreams in the foregoing chapters, the behavior of the dreamers and the people appearing in the dreams was not too unusual. However, the dream in which the woman who put her children in the theater cloakroom (page 46) and then forgot them shows extraordinarily unusual behavior for a mother. When one realizes, however, that children stood in the way of her career, one can easily understand how such a dream could appear, even if the dreamer is not psychotic, but only quite neurotic.

Powerful archetypal material often indicates that the person is in danger from unconscious contents. Often the engulfing or flooding has already happened and the condition of the person expresses this clearly in reality: for example, in the dream of the oak trees (page 49-50) which were in danger of being destroyed from a quick-spreading disease. Still, the man's reaction in the dream and in the following sessions indicated that he was able to react with appropriate feelings to the situation. In addition he urgently asked for help. That made the diagnosis and prognosis better than if he had not had such a reaction.

Further, it is important that one does not commit oneself to a diagnosis after the first few dreams, but observes over a longer period to be sure that no important aspects have been overlooked. That happens automatically during treatment, through the constant reference to dreams that act as a barometer for the counselor.

The counselor must also observe manifestations of the shadow, where the least integrated functions reside. In the dream in which the mother of the newly wed young woman stands at the foot of the bed (page 84), she is the shadow. One could say that, regarding her sexual relationship to her husband, the wife is living the shadow of the mother. In the dream of the man with the homosexual problem (page 58), the dog infected with silverfish was the man's shadow: he symbolized a sexually undifferentiated side. With this dream, although no sexual act was performed in it, the man became conscious of his sexual problem. Dogs often symbolize primitive, instinctive behavior.

The therapist draws the greatest certainty as to the effectiveness of treatment from dreams that immediately follow a counseling session. The dreams of the young woman who slowly freed herself from her mother show in what ways the detachment took place: first as an adolescent rebellion, later as a peaceful burial of the mother (pages 85-86). When they have been worked through, the shadow aspects often leave in a friendly way or are buried. If the shadow is done away with in a brutal and dramatic way—perhaps through murder—that indicates a need to repress the problem quickly and forcefully. One can be sure that a shadow done away with like that will reappear until a genuine working through of the problem has taken place.

Naturally much more could be read from all of these dreams. The more one sees, the better the counseling proceeds. In the chapter on Mark and Debbie, the attempt was made to show the varied relationships between daily life and the dreams that followed.

Dreams are not only of use during diagnosis and treatment, but are also especially helpful in the concluding phase of therapy. Discussions of the right time to end therapy can cause tension, especially if the partners want to stop too soon according to the counselor. The reverse sometimes occurs, when the couple wants to keep the support of the group or therapist longer than seems appropriate to the therapist. Tension is eased considerably if the couple and the therapist allow the dream to play a role in deciding either for or against ending therapy.

Different criteria should be considered before one decides to end counseling: the dream should end in a positive way; the dream's suggested solution should give rise to a harmonious emotional response in the dreamer and point toward achieving a homeostatic balance. The ego should appear strengthened; the anima or animus relationship should be positive. In addition, the feeling reaction of the dreamer in the dream and increasingly in reality should appear reasonable.

These conditions were not met in the case of the older couple described in chapter six who believed their problems had been pretty well resolved so that they could stop therapy. The restless man who had eight moons in his heaven (page 84) was still far from a normalization of his extraverted behavior. His wife, who had become overly anxious about middle age and death, needed to strengthen her ego function considerably before she would be able to deal with her problems with more equanimity.

The dream that showed in the most unequivocal way what one could hope for from a dream at the end of therapy was that of the young couple who were caught in the tangle of sexual conflict. The dream in which they ride on a bicycle-built-for-two (page 85) showed a well-balanced trend and the baby sitting between them symbolized the new life in their marriage. The anima-animus relationship and the complement of two voices in a duet (pages 63-64) correspond to the balance one wishes for from a "final" dream.

Although the case of Mark and Debbie, which took place over several months, was only described briefly, it should be enough to understand better the interlocking aspect of the conscious and the unconscious. The connections between the symbols of a dream, the behavior in daily life, and the response of the next dream to that behavior, provides practical insight into the value of working with dreams.

This book is primarily concerned with the use of dreams in couple counseling; nevertheless I'd like to add some general advice for the counselor: advice for premarital counseling of couples, considerations for the first interview, suggestions for establishing rapport, and different points of view for the three phases of treatment—beginning, middle and end. Finally I will give a few guidelines for counselors in their role as group leaders.

Premarital Counseling

Young couples frequently come to premarital counseling on the advice of clergy or their parents, not because these people disapprove of the proposed marriage, but because they would like to give the young couple another chance to examine themselves thoroughly. I think premarital counseling is an unusually helpful process that more young couples should take advantage of. Even short-term groups that meet for three or four sessions have proven worthwhile.

Attention must be paid to the shadow side of each partner in premarital counseling, as well as to the ways in which each person deals with his or her own and the partner's problems. Expectations of the marriage, the partner and oneself must be examined critically, especially in terms of whether they are realistic.

Tom and Elli, for example (page 73), could have been spared much trouble if they had discussed their problems before the marriage. When time allows, one can also say something about the typology of each partner, educating them to the advantages and disadvantages of each type and how they can best communicate.

The First Interview

In the first interview one should learn just why the couple has decided to begin counseling at this time. In large part the answers can be divided into three categories. The first answer is the following: "I've been wanting to go to a marriage counselor for years." This type of person would rather solve his or her problems alone and feels that it is degrading to seek help from others. This kind of person is even reluctant to seek medical help sometimes. The opposite type runs to a marriage counselor at the first big fight, assuming that the partner—not oneself—needs help. This kind of person tries to win over the marriage counselor as an ally in order to bring some insight to the partner, the one who must change. A third kind of advice-seeker sees the marriage counselor as a kind of demigod who will make everything right.

Asking questions about their reasons for coming gives the counselor clues to the couple's relationship. Does one of them speak for the other? Does one constantly contradict the other? Does the answer to the question lead to an argument or to sarcastic comments? That and more become apparent in connection with a harmless question in the first interview.

Rapport

In order to establish good rapport—a prerequisite for any counseling—it is helpful to suggest to the couple that they not discuss the counseling sessions at home as this often leads to arguments. Instead they should keep a journal and note down problems and observations. They should also write down their dreams, making special note of dates. In this way the couple will gain some distance from each other, become calmer and start on a new course to deal with their problems. Sometimes the tension in the relationship is so great that this advice can't be followed, but even this helps the counselor to gain a greater understanding of the partners and their conflicts.

Now and again I have been asked whether dreams are sometimes written down in a distorted way. Perhaps the dreamer censors them in order to appear in a better light or because a certain part of the dream is painful. This is often the case in the beginning if sexual material or a criticism of the counselor is involved. However, it's not important whether the dream is written down truthfully, because the censorship or the enhanced self-image in itself says something decisive about the dreamer.

Once the counselor accepts the couple, he or she will try to create a calm atmosphere. Since one is dealing with two people who may disagree about many things, this often causes difficulty. The job is made easier if the counselor leads the sessions with another counselor of the opposite sex, so that they can speak with each about the positive and negative feelings that arise in relation to the couple. Of course no one is completely free of projections, but two therapists are able to balance each other and observe if one or the other begins to take sides.

In the beginning it is important to help the partners listen to each other. A good idea is for each person to say one or two sentences and then for the other to repeat back what was heard. At first, it is almost impossible. Instead of repeating verbatim what the other said, he or she usually offers an unfriendly version such as, "I knew he was going to say that . . ." or "That's how she always is— criticize, criticize!" If, after some time, one is actually able to get each one to repeat what the other said and then to express how that makes him or her feel, the complaints and arguments are often reduced.

At this point the counselor can ask the couple what they had originally both hoped for in the marriage—how they saw their partner and themselves. Such an approach leads to their own shadow sides and is more fruitful than dealing with the negative qualities of the other.

At the beginning the counselor, together with the couple, will formulate a realistic goal concerning the length of counseling and what can probably be achieved in the given time. The couple's reaction to this suggestion is often reflected in their dreams. Through discussions of expectations for the treatment, the beginning of a transference between the counselor and the couple brings to light the positive and negative projections of the couple onto the counselors. Dreams always serve to acquaint the counselor with the state of the transference. For example, the negative transference in the dream in which I overfed the patient with chicken (page 56) was quite revealing. Likewise, the dream with snooping "Aunt Neil" (page 68) made clear that, at the moment, I stood for a snoop who wanted to coax the patient's secret out of her.

Whether the counseling is of short or long duration, whether it consists of individual or group sessions, the dreams remain for three-quarters of the treatment the barometer not only for the transference situation, but even more, for progress or regression in the therapy. Almost every dream confronts the dreamer with a central problem, be it the dog with the silverfish (page 58) or Hanna's animus, which first freed her from the subway train (page 61) and later became a vital young man with whom she sang a duet (page 64). Another example would be the innumerable dreams of Clark and Leslie that confronted them with the self-destructive nature of their intentions every time they wanted to return to the marriage.

Final Phase of Therapy

In the final phase of counseling it is important that the counselor help the couple become aware that, no matter what decision has been made, it has both advantages and disadvantages. As with every decision in life, one must have some idea of the price to be paid. The question is not how beautiful and good everything will be from then on, but what tasks life will bring as a result. The question is this: Do I have the strength to take on this task, to carry this kind of burden? A better marriage means being able to work on oneself and lending strength to one's partner when necessary. It means a commitment to the possible in the relationship instead of expecting the impossible.

Separation or divorce is only unavoidable when one of the partners either can't or won't change. (Clark is an example.) Sometimes the difference in personality type is so great that the price of adjustment is too high. This is, however, seldom the case. In Chuck's and Joan's case it was quite possible to build a bridge between his introversion and her extraversion so that their opposite types would complement each other.

The dreams that occur at the end of counseling are usually more positive than those at the beginning. They show less conflict and more balance; they're less dramatic, almost boring. The behavior of people in the dreams is closer to real life. Bizarre images and happenings have almost disappeared. The "I" of the dream behaves appropriately, so there are no walks on subway tracks (page 52) and no attempts to seduce men in Times Square wearing nothing but a black bikini (page 90).

Transference

At the end of therapy it is imperative for the counselor to resolve the transference, that is, the dependence of the couple on the counselor, and also to work through his or her own countertransference, an exaggerated feeling-toned interest in the couple. Otherwise the counselor becomes like a worried parent who wants to protect the clients from all difficulties and believes that "the children" just can't make it alone. When a couple and the counselor are free of their parent-child roles, they then face each other as equals, as self-sufficient adults.

Counseling in a Group

Naturally dreams occupy a much more central part in individual therapy and can be explored in greater depth than in a group. However, groups offer a kind of shared experience and support, as well as confrontation, with others who are in a similar situation.

There is no general rule as to how long one should keep the partners in individual therapy before bringing them into a group. It is important to be sure that each person is able to stand confrontation. There are times in every group when the leader must step in and shield a member from an attack that is too harsh. That is different from an individual who is still hurting too much to expose him- or herself to a group at all.

In addition to the considerations already mentioned, the following are also important: The counselor should monitor the group and take care that the interactions among the members remains lively.

Nothing is more disheartening and anxiety provoking than a group that sits there in weary silence. There are certain ways to avoid this circumstance and it is useful for the counselor and the group members to learn them.

1. Hiding Places

I take it for granted that people who come to a group for the first time are afraid. They don't want the others to see that and they don't want to be attacked. Therefore they protect themselves. "I'm not going to make a fool of myself with my opinions," the newcomer thinks. He expresses himself carefully and politely when he says, "I think we would all like to help you!" The group leader should step in immediately and suggest to the newcomer that he say "I" instead of "we." "Okay," says the newcomer, "I would like to help you." He senses right away that he feels more insecure when he says "I" instead of "we."

Again and again the counselor must remind the members that it is more honest for each person to speak for him- or herself instead of for the whole group or the whole world as, for example, "One simply can't let that happen." Concealed in that approach is a safe hiding place, an attempt to avoid responsibility for one's own opinion. When the speaker says, "I can't let that happen," he stands alone with his idea. No one supports him. Some group members could possibly confront him. He is exposed when he says "I" instead of "we," "one" or "each." In a group one can learn to take responsibility for what one feels.

2. Talking to others, not about them

Another way of evading responsibility is avoiding speaking directly to someone; for example, "Tom only hears what he wants to hear," or, "That always struck me about Tom also." In this situation the counselor should make the wife aware that Tom is sitting in the circle and that she should speak *to* him rather than *about* him.

This is not just a formality. When the group members talk *about*

Tom they don't need to interact with him directly; in fact, he is hardly even present and can't therefore answer to them. He becomes an object of gossip and therefore not dangerous. In such a case, the counselor should turn to Tom and ask him, "What do you feel when your wife talks about you as though you're not even here?" The interaction of the group is based on bringing the most personal feelings and wishes out into the open. When necessary, the group leader intervenes to help members own their feelings and also to change them.

3. Excursions

Various kinds of "excursions" are also a way to flee interaction: recollections of childhood with long tales about parents; long-past stories of illnesses or an almost forgotten first marriage; excursions into the workplace with detailed descriptions of bosses or colleagues. Most group members are glad to go along either as silent listeners or active participants.

The appeal of such digressions is obvious: The speaker wants to impress the group with what a good person he or she is and how unfair life is. Above all, the person wants to avoid grappling with present problems. In a tacit understanding each one supports the other in ignoring the here and now and enjoying the harmless gossip which takes some of the strain off of the seriousness of the group situation.

The group leader will allow these escape attempts only as long as they seem useful, perhaps even to the point where the participants themselves become bored, or the conversation slowly comes to a standstill, and each member wonders, surprised, what has happened and why everything has become so quiet.

4. Scapegoating

"Excursions" are especially worthwhile if they unearth a scapegoat from the past: "My mother never liked me . . ." "If my parents hadn't favored my younger brother over myself, I wouldn't be here today; they're to blame for everything." "My boss is like my father—stupid and stubborn. It's no wonder I can't stand it!" The group is like the chorus in a Greek drama. They're angry with the mother of the group member; they damn the stubborn father or boss, thus offering the solidarity of scapegoat hunters. Such accusations divert attention from the group member's own responsibilities.

From there it is only a small step to discovering a scapegoat in the group. People who were scapegoats in childhood unconsciously constellate that role in the group. The couple counselor has to do some important work in explaining this. The pursuer and the pursued must become conscious of their behavior. Pursuing and attacking don't lead to genuine confrontation. Those being attacked become anxious and will avoid talking in the group or they will stay away altogether. Those pursuing learn nothing from their aggressive behavior. They're just happy that they have found someone on whom to project their own negativity.

In this way the group comes by a sense of superiority very cheaply. The group members avoid the self-confrontation that is necessary for personal growth. The counselor steps in at this point to hold up to the group a mirror that reflects the fact that their weaknesses are not so different from those of the scapegoat.

Before someone can be turned into a scapegoat, people have to take sides—judge and condemn. Usually the group isn't even aware how the witch-hunt begins. In any case, it doesn't take long for the group to develop a sense of solidarity. The entire group isn't always involved; it also happens that one member will open the attack by provoking another member. This could happen more or less as follows:

Al: "I find your behavior unbelievable."
Bert (stammering): "How I behave has nothing to do with you."
Al: "What are you doing here if you don't want to change?"
Bert: "That doesn't concern you either."
Cecilie (Bert's wife): "Why do you put up with that?"

If Bert is very defensive, that kind of talk could continue and come to a head in an ever more aggressive way. If Bert is rather timid, he could become furious at the group and leave, full of unacknowledged anxiety. Such a dialogue precludes group interaction and doesn't help the one affected. Once again the counselor must intervene and try to turn the accusations into a meaningful dialogue, perhaps by suggesting that Al express his feelings about Bert's behavior. Newcomers to a group are often not aware that they have trouble expressing feelings, particularly when they are aggressive. Al might answer, "I just told him what I feel—I find his behavior unbelievable!"

Counselor: "That is an accusation, a judgment, but it tells me nothing about what you are feeling when you say that Bert's behavior is "unbelievable."

Al: "But it's clear—I'm outraged."

Now the counselor can call on Al to say precisely why Bert's behavior so infuriates him but not the other group members. When Al is finally able to get hold of himself again and realizes how aggressive his feelings are, the door is open for a productive expression of feeling. Naturally the counselor tries to bring Bert out of his rigid defensiveness by asking him what he felt when Al attacked him. Was he afraid? Did he feel superior? Angry? Misunderstood? What does he feel now when he hears how even Al and the others are talking about the insecurity that provoked their aggression?

Al: "Yeah, if I felt more secure I wouldn't be so aggressive. I always feel that I have to be on my guard so that someone else doesn't attack me first."

Now Al and Bert could talk to each other calmly. It could even be worthwhile for the group leader to have the two members of the group who irritate each other make a so-called "contract." Bert would ask Al, "What are you afraid of now?" when Al begins to get aggressive. He would call on Al to talk freely about his feelings and would help him as well as he could. Al would ask Bert the same questions whenever Bert began to lie and to stutter (Bert's defensive tactics when he is afraid).

It is more difficult for a couple to form such a "contract." Feelings are too deep-seated to be cleared up quickly by talking about them. It is appropriate to interrupt the argument and to ask, "Bert, do you hear how your voice sounds? You're also jiggling your foot angrily." His wife, Cecilie, and the rest of the group also chime in with comments about how his voice sounds. Now it is up to Cecilie to say how she feels when Bert adopts this tone. "I'm afraid whenever he gets so angry," she said. "And what do you feel?" the counselor asked the husband.

These situations between partners or between individual group members repeat themselves in hundreds of variations. Therefore it is important time and again to point out to the participants how they speak to and hear the others. They should not only become aware of the tone and content of their reproaches, but also learn to pay attention to body language—the folded arms, the jiggling foot, avoidance of eye contact. They should try to be aware of their own feelings when they react vehemently, shyly or sarcastically.

The most important thing for partners to learn is to listen to each other. In the early weeks they just wait for the other to pause for breath so they can let loose with a new accusation. It takes a surprisingly long time until group members understand the difference between accusations and stating one's feelings.

5. The Difference between Hostility and Anger

"No, I wouldn't want to be married to you. You're a regular harridan!" Behind such a statement may lie the feeling, "I get so mad when you talk to your husband in such a hostile way. It reminds me of my parents. I would like to step in and put a stop to it."

Anger is always contained in aggression, but it leads to different group interaction when members express their feelings directly instead of indirectly. Some people have trouble grasping the difference between hostility and anger. Anger is a genuine emotion that people bring into a discussion. Hostility only wounds without adding clarity.

Counselors need a lot of patience, especially in the first ten sessions or so. They may need to step in and remind group members, "And what do you feel when . . ." They should pull back, however, as soon as at least some of the group members become aware that condemnation and hostility are gaining the upper hand. As soon as the group is able to point out to each other that it is better to express feelings than to pass judgment, that anger is a genuine and acceptable feeling, while hostility falls under the heading of condemnation, then the group leader can leave the interaction to the group.

6. *Giving Advice*

Taking sides leads to judgment and condemnation, but so does well-meaning advice. It is useless to say, "If I were in your place . . . ," because "I" is always a completely different person than the one being advised. What seems easy and is right for one person may be completely wrong, if not impossible, for another.

Most of the advice given in counseling and in the group is already familiar to the one seeking advice. He or she is just not able to act on it for psychological reasons. For example, if Hanna, who is of average height and weighs about two hundred pounds, asks, "Do you know of a good diet for losing weight?" everybody answers with suggestions. I don't say anything and now she turns to me. I answer, "Maybe we could talk about whether you could keep to one of these diets. We could talk about where your difficulty lies." If a corresponding dream is available, Hanna could listen to the advice of her own unconscious.

Sometimes someone will talk in great detail about the acute difficulties in a relationship. The group then feels that advice and help are appropriate. As stated above, some offer advice that will never be applied. Some are very uneasy and quiet because they don't have advice to give and yet feel a duty to try to help. Once again the group leader has something important to teach: that expressing their feelings about what they have heard is the biggest help of all.

For example, Leslie had talked about an unpleasant scene with Clark and she thought there was no way out of the situation.

Hanna followed the unconscious request for advice with a question, "Why don't you get a divorce?"

"That might be too big a step," said Hilda, "but a temporary separation would surely help both of you."

Elli, who was sitting next to Leslie, took her hand spontaneously and said, "I'm really sad that I can't help. I like you so much and all of this makes me very sad."

Leslie started crying and we all had the feeling that it would do her good to cry and release some tension. When she could talk again Leslie said, "I'm so afraid to leave Clark and live alone."

The help she had needed was to have someone take her hand and show her genuine sympathy.

Martin wanted to change jobs but didn't know if the new possibility was better than the existing one. In a breathless monologue he talked of the advantages and disadvantages of his present job and the possible new one. His way of speaking became faster and more and more monotonous.

"I'm sorry, Martin," said his wife, "but I can't stand it anymore; you sound like a machine gun. I'd like to help you, but I can't listen any more."

Martin was taken aback and stopped talking.

"You've thrown so many facts and figures at us that I'm completely confused," said Fred. "What do you feel about the change? Do you like your old workplace? How about your boss? Tell us something about that!"

Then Martin told how much he liked his place of work, even the set-up in the laboratory, including the view from the window. He liked his boss very much, but recently he had become afraid that a new employee could edge him out. "Wouldn't you feel better if you could talk this over with your boss?" asked John.

Martin nodded, "Yeah, I think I'll do that." No longer did he talk like a machine gun. He looked at the group and said, "Thanks," as if relieved.

This is usually the case. A spontaneous expression of feeling is of more help than advice, no matter how intelligent.

7. Questions

Accusations, judgments and advice are undesirable for the purposes of the group process because they are unproductive and hamper group interaction. All three—accuser, judge and advice-giver—step out of relationship and seek a position of superiority instead, in which they are well guarded against the accusations and judgments of others.

Too many questions and ready answers can damage the quality of group interaction. Therefore, at a certain moment, John advised a member of the group not to ask a question, but to make a statement. That sounds strange. Why shouldn't someone ask a question? Isn't that natural when one wants to know something? It may be natural, but it doesn't lead to dialogue. Question and answer are a form of interrogation; at best, one uses them during an interview.

Most of us have unpleasant memories of situations in which we had to justify ourselves while being questioned. For instance parents asked, "Where were you for so long?" Or there were questions from teachers, from the police, from one's superiors in the workplace—questions that weren't really questions, but disguised accusations. A seemingly joking question such as, "Late again?" is actually an accusation. The reaction to it is either an intellectual explanation or a defensive answer.

However, if one follows John's advice and changes the question to a statement expressing the feeling that the late arrival arouses, then one creates a feeling of solidarity. One can say, "I always get angry when you arrive too late. I can't concentrate when everyone isn't here on time." If the person spoken to addresses the feeling of the speaker, then the response is no longer defensive. "You won't believe it," he might admit, "but I react in exactly the same way. It's terrible, but I have a problem with time." An exchange took place here; a dialogue between equals.

Questions that contain blame expose someone; they wound and make the person asking into an authoritarian. Other questions can hinder a productive exchange in the group and lessen the possibility of getting to know one another. "Do you have any children?" "Where are you going this summer?" "Why don't you answer your husband?" These are completely harmless questions. The answers to these and a hundred other harmless questions are one word or a short sentence; then another question follows. Even when other group members join in with a few questions the whole thing is rather boring.

The group leader shouldn't let things come to this point. She or he should step in and call on the speaker to make a statement and to declare the reason for the question. This is difficult for almost everyone at first. Later it goes without saying. "I would like to know whether you have children," a group member said. "I had the impression that you and your wife do many interesting things together. You have a lot of free time. We couldn't do that with our three children." Or: "Where are you going this summer? Well, it isn't really important to me where you're going. I only asked because I'd like to talk to you." That is a real invitation to a conversation. The third person now said, "It makes me mad when you don't answer your husband, but it also angers me that he lets you get away with it." If the speaker is now asked to look for a reason why the behavior of the other couple is so disturbing, some interesting material will probably come to light.

As already mentioned, one can comfortably hide behind questions and feel superior. But making a statement also implies accepting responsibility and opening oneself up to the possibility of criticism. Instead of showing the other up, he or she is exposed by stating underlying motives. This goes for the counselor as well as for group members. Whenever possible, the counselor should voice observations and feelings rather than ask questions.

The most important rule for couple counselors and group members is to avoid everything that hampers interaction and to do all one can to foster a lively exchange. As long as the counselor has an educational effect on the group and supports a productive group process, progress will come. To the extent that the group learns and applies the "rules of the game" and takes over responsibility for interaction, then the counselor can step back and be there just in case.

At this stage participants can go more deeply into the interpersonal tensions in the group and turn to the inner conflicts and dreams of individuals.

An Interview with Dr. Renée Nell
By Antoinette Bosco
(from *The Litchfield County Times,* January 1, 1993)

Sitting in the living room of her home, Dr. Renée Nell recalled a dream she had half a century ago that literally changed her life.

"The dream was in a foreign language, one I didn't know. But I remembered one sentence and when I woke up, I wrote it down," related Dr. Nell, who at that time lived in California working as a screenwriter. She decided to ask a professor friend if he was in any way familiar with this language, although it seemed to her to be just gibberish.

"To my surprise, he told me it was Aramaic, a language from 2,000 years back. And he gave me the translation, which was something like, 'Don't try to be more than yourself.'

"It was amazing," she went on. "At the time, I needed to slough off a lot of things . . . to get closer to myself, be simpler, to find myself." Born a Jew in Germany, she had lived through the trauma of the Nazi terror, which had destroyed her parents and beloved relatives. Under horrendous circumstances, she made her way through Switzerland to America, eventually working in a profession that, she knew down deep, was not what she really wanted.

"With that dream, I found something," said Dr. Nell, who had already served an apprenticeship of sorts with the noted psychiatrist, Dr. Carl Jung, at the University of Zurich. It was that she should pursue a career as a psychotherapist, with a focus on dream analysis, because she had come to see that "the dream is the mirror of the problem, and the answer to it," she explained.

As for why the dream's message "was in a language I didn't understand," Dr. Nell referred to what Dr. Jung had said, "that we also find in the unconscious qualities that are not individually acquired but are inherited." Since Aramaic was a Semitic language spoken in

148

ancient Biblical times, she speculated that her dream may have been somehow linked to her Jewish roots.

Her dream had told her that "it was not all that complex" to cut away the excesses and choose the path that could led to that healing profession which she realized "would never bore me," said Dr. Nell. So, "paying attention" to her unconscious, thanks to that dream, the sophisticated young woman decided to return to her studies with Dr. Jung and then went on to earn a doctorate at Columbia University. She affirmed that dream analysis has remained "fascinating, always a challenging mystery. I feel like a detective." And, she quipped, "I've met people who bored me, but never a dream that bored me."

Dr. Nell founded and directed The Country Place in Litchfield, Connecticut, a residential mental health. She wrote books on children's, mother's and father's dreams, as well as a book on the use of dreams in marriage counseling. Ask anyone who has sought help from Dr. Nell with understanding a dream; they will tell you that she has a gift for it.

Asked why it is so difficult to remember or interpret dreams, she shrugged. "There's no reason why you should remember them. Our mind works very economically. However, when there is a reason to remember a dream, people do, and then it is important to pay attention," she said, pointing out that most people need help with interpreting their dreams. "If something in your life is unbalanced, the dream quickly tells you. The dream always tries to guide you to honest balance. If you're not in a spiritual relationship with yourself, you're in a shadow, and the dream always brings up the shadow.

"Often the dream is pushing you to do the positive thing you are not doing . . . because you are not conscious of your resistance, When you go against your unconscious, this begins to speak louder and louder until you have a nightmare. It's the unconscious saying, 'listen to me, you dumb thing!'" If the dream is understood, one finds immediate help with the problem. And Dr. Nell says that what she trusts most in getting to the core meaning of the dream is the Jungian approach.

"Jung says that dreams mean exactly what they say. If you dream about a factory chimney, it's a factory chimney and not a penis," she commented, alluding to what might be a Freudian approach. "In Jung's terms, the dream is like a story; there are no free associations . . . and all aspects are oneself."

According to Dr. Nell, "the first sentence of the dream gives you the theme and the rest is the working out, with the last paragraph summing up what should be done about the problem. It gives you a solution, a warning, or advice.

"I ask for the dream to be boiled down to three sentences," Dr. Nell went on, explaining how she uses the Jungian approach. "Then I ask, what happened the day before, or, if the dream refers to something in your past, what was going on in that time of your life. You see, you want to get to why you had the dream now and not last week, and what it wants to tell you." For example, she described the woman who dreamed about a squeaky staircase. This dream occurred after a phone call from her mother-in-law wanting something from her. The dreamer is staircase. "Everybody is using her; she's complaining, 'squeaking.' Her dream is saying 'let's stop you from being a squeaky staircase.'"

In another instance, a person dreams, "I'm in my Volkswagen, on a roller coaster. My car jumps the tracks, speeds downhill and crashes into a wall." Dr. Nell continues, "I didn't have to know how old she was or what her babyhood was like," as may be the case with therapies that do not work with dreams. "I knew she was in acute danger of crashing. The immediate problem had to do with what was her thing with speed. She knew the answer—she was always in a rush," Dr. Nell said, commenting on how the dream was revealing the warning from her unconscious, that if she continued rushing, she was in danger of being out of control.

"You see, the dream functions on the psychological level the same as the body functions on the physical level. It tells us nonverbally if we're doing something wrong. For instance, if you eat bad food, the body tells you—not with words, but with the attempt to restore balance and so, you vomit. Dreams do the same, they're not very verbal," she said, further explaining that being "normal" means to be in balance, "living with the dictates of your body instead of against; and living psychologically in harmony with yourself."

Dr. Nell affirmed, "To me, the dream talks so clearly. It is sometimes clearer than what a client tells me. The dream always tries to guide you to honest balance."

Because dreams come from such a deep, personal place, Dr. Nell puts little stock in books trying to explain dream symbols. "You can't take a symbol by itself. You need the association of the person. For example, if you dream about rain, for one person this might mean fertility, but for another, flooding."

She also expressed deep negative feelings about so-called "lucid dreaming," where "they're now trying to train people to manipulate their dreams. That's terrible. Dreams are the only thing left where we don't have to be manipulated," she stated firmly.

Dr. Nell has given more than half a century to her psychological work with people suffering from psychological disorders, committed to the belief that "they need total therapy for the whole person." Even now she is far from retired. After selling The Country Place, she started The Litchfield Guidance Center to offer therapeutic and referral services to individuals and families in emotional distress, regardless of their financial situation.

Bibliography

Cohn, R.C. "The Theme-Centered Interactional Method, Group Therapists as Group Educators." In *The Journal of Group Psychoanalysis and Process 2* (1969-70).

Eidelberg, L. *Neurotic Interaction in Marriage.* New York: Basic Books, 1956.

Hall, James A. *Jungian Dream Interpretation: A Handbook of Theory and Practice.* Toronto: Inner City Books, 1983.

Hollis, James. *The Eden Project: In Search of the Magical Other.* Toronto: Inner City Books, 1998.

Jung, C.G. *The Collected Works* (Bollingen Series XX). 20 vols. Trans. R.F.C. Hull. Ed. H. Read, M. Fordham, G. Adler, Wm. McGuire. Princeton: Princeton University Press, 1953-1979.

Jung, Emma. *Animus and Anima: Two Essays.* Woodstock, CT: Spring Publications, 1985.

Nell, Renée. "Guidance Through Dreams." In *Ways of Growth,* New York: Grossman Inc., 1968.

_____. "The Use of Dreams in Couples Group Therapy." In *National Alliance for Family Life,* vol. 3, no. 2 (1975).

Sharp, Daryl. *Personality Types: Jung's Model of Typology.* Toronto: Inner City Books, 1987.

_____. *Digesting Jung: Food for the Journey.* Toronto: Inner City Books, 2001.

_____. *Jung Lexicon: A Primer of Terms and Concepts.* Toronto: Inner City Books, 1991.

Singer, June. *Boundaries of the Soul.* New York: Doubleday, 1972.

Young-Eisendrath, Polly. *Hags and Heroes: A Feminist Approach to Jungian Therapy with Couples.* Toronto: Inner City Books, 1984.

Index

Entries in *italics* refer to illustrations

accomplishment, 25
accusations, 145
active vs. passive behaviour, 122-123
adolescence, 16-17
advice, 111-112, 143-144
aggression, 10-11, 18, 39, 128, 140-142
alcoholism, 79-80, 106-107
analytical psychology, 9. *See also* Jung,
    C.G./Jungian
anger and hostility, 142-143
anima, 13-16, 58, 60, 67-68, 88-89, 126-
    127, 129, 132
animal(s), 12
    in dreams, 39, 54
animus, 13, 15-16, 58, 60-61, 64, 80-81,
    98-99, 126-127, 132
apathy, 53
archetypal/archetype(s), 12-13
    dreams, 12-13, 130
attitudinal opposites, 35, 37
aunt in attic, dream of, 68-69, 82, 129, 136
Aunt Margaret, dream of, 10-12, 128-129

baby, dream of, 85-86, 117-119, 132. *See*
    also children
balance, 9
balloon flight, dream of, 124
behavior, 21, 130, 132, 137
    active vs. passive, 122-123
being killed, dream of, 108-110
being late, dream of, 125
bicycle-built-for-two, dream of, 85, 132
Bill and Jenny, 27-31
body in dreams, 20, 52
brain creatures, dream of, 120
brother singing, dream of, 88
burden, true and false, 100-101

canceled marriage, dream of, 121
car(s), 90
    dream of, 21
castle in the air, dream of, 94-95
celebrating mass, dream of, 9-10
censorship of dreams, 134-135
chicken, dream of, 56-57, 136
children, dream of, 46, 54, 130. *See also*
    baby
Chuck and Joan, 38-40, 81
Clark and Leslie, 66, 70-81, 87-110
clothing, 16-17, 40, 128
colleague, counseling with a, 41-42, 44-45,
    135
collective unconscious, 11-13
college, dream of, 97-99
communication, 111
conflict(s), 8, 24
confrontation from dreams, 34
conscious(ness), 20, 23, 132
contract in therapy, 141-142
coolies, dream of, 24-25
counseling,, advice in, 111-112
    dreams in, 7-8, 112
    final stages of, 83-113
    goals in, 111, 135
    taking sides in, 100-101, 103-104, 113,
        135
    with a colleague, 41-42, 44-45, 135
crippled men, dream of, 31-33

dancing in the street, dream of, 90-91
danger, dream of, 21
Debbie and Mark, 114-125
deflation of ego, 21-22
diagnosis based on dreams, 44, 47, 49, 51-
    52, 54, 129-131
Diane and Fred, 45-48

digressions in group therapy, 139
diseased tree, dream of, 49-50, 130
divorce, 101-102, 112-113, 136
dog(s), dream of, 58-59, 64, 93-94, 131
dream(s), 7-8, 18, 21, 23, 25-27, 33, 39,
        104, 112, 126-127, 132, 135-136
    anima/animus in, 14, 16, 88-89, 129
    of animals, 39, 54
    archetypal, 12-13, 130
    of aunt in attic, 68-69, 82, 129, 136
    of Aunt Margaret, 10-12, 128-129
    of baby, 85-86, 117-119, 132. See also
        dream(s) of children
    of balloon flight, 124
    behavior in, 130, 137
    of being killed, 108-110
    of being late, 125
    of bicycle-built-for-two, 85, 132
    body in, 20
    of brain creatures, 120
    of brother singing, 88
    of cancelled marriage, 121
    of car, 21
    of castle in the air, 94-96
    of celebrating mass, 9-10
    censorship of, 134-135
    of chicken, 56-57, 135
    of children, 46, 54, 130. See also
        dream(s) of baby
    clothing in, 128
    of college, 97-99
    confrontation from, 34
    of coolies, 24-25
    of crippled men, 31-33
    of dancing in the street, 90-91
    of danger, 21
    diagnosis based on, 44, 47, 49, 51-52,
        54, 129-131
    of diseased tree, 49-50, 130
    of dog(s), 58-59, 64, 93-94, 131
    of duet, 63-64, 81, 132
    ego in, 19, 52, 128, 130, 132, 137

    of factory, 43-44, 52, 130
    of fall, 84
    of "Familia," 125
    of Faulkner, 104-106
    feeling in, 132
    of films, 71-72
    in final stages of counseling, 83-113,
        131-132, 136-137
    of flying, 66-68, 129
    following counseling sessions, 131
    of forgetting children, 46, 54, 130
    of freezer, 117-118
    God in, 128
    of gold box, 24-25
    in group therapy, 79-82
    of haunted house, 97-99
    of house, 89, 95-100
    of husband who leaves, 75-78, 80
    of identity, 73, 80-81
    interpretation of, 10-11, 25-26, 54-55,
        127-128
    of intestines, 107-108
    Jung on, 9-10, 25-26
    of killing women, 92-93
    of ladder, 17
    message of the, 80
    of monsters, 124
    of moons, 84, 132
    of mother, 84-86, 131. See also
        dream(s), of parents
    of operation, 120
    of parent(s), 62-63, 82. See also
        dream(s), of parents
    partners and, 81
    of party, 38-40, 54, 129
    of penholder, 10
    persona in, 128
    of pool, 89
    of power, 104-107
    for prognosis, 8, 44, 47-48, 130-131
    of psychiatrists, 95-96
    psychosis as shown in, 52-53, 130

of public speaking, 73-74
responsibility for content of, 11
of ringing telephone, 83-84
of Rita, 88-89
same gender person in, 128
Self in, 24, 128
self in, 19. See also dream(s), ego in
of separated woman, 97-98
shadow in, 39, 129, 131
of sinister character, 18-19
structure of, 26, 127
of subway, 61
of superior, 125
and termination of therapy, 82
of tower, 38-39, 54, 66-68, 129
of tree disease, 49-50, 130
of two women, 71-72
of voice, 121
    of God, 23-24
of weaving, 13
of wife eating arm, 28-29, 129
of wild horse, 124
duet, dream of, 63-64, 81, 132

ego, 16, 19-25, 52, 128, 130, 132, 137
Elli and Tom, 66-67, 84-87, 100, 133
empathy with last speaker, 7-8
Eric and Hanna, 57-64, 78-79, 81-82
Erwin and Lotte, 83-84
excursions in group therapy, 139
extraversion/extravert, 34-37, 129, 136

factory, dream of, 43-44, 52, 130
fairy tales, 12
fall, dream of, 84
false and true burden, 100-101
"Familia," dream of, 125
Faulkner, dream of, 104-106
feeling, 132, 143-144
film(s), dream of, 71-73
final stages of counseling, 137
    dreams in, 83-113, 131-132, 136

first interview, 133-134
flying dream of, 66-68, 129
forgetting children, dream of, 46, 54, 130
Fred and Diane, 45-48
freezer, dream of, 117-118

gender in dreams, 128
goals in counseling, 111, 135
God, in dreams, 23-24, 128
    gold box, dream of, 24-25
group therapy, 39-42, 65-82, 137-142, 146

Hanna and Eric, 57-64, 78-79, 81-82
haunted house, dream of, 97-99
Herman and Mary, 42-45, 110-111
hiding places in group therapy, 138
Hilda and Martin, 65-69, 78-79, 82
hostility and anger, 142-143
house, dream of, 89, 95-100
husband who leaves, dream of, 75-78, 80

"I" in dreams. *See* ego
identity, dream of, 73, 80-81
individual vs. group therapy, 137
individuality, 17
individuation, 9, 25, 128
inflation, 21-22
instinct/instinctive, 12
interpretation of dreams, 10-11, 25-26, 54-
    55, 127-128
intestines, dream of, 107-108
introvert/introversion, 34-37, 129, 136

Jenny and Bill, 27-31
Joan and Chuck, 38-40, 81
journal, 134
Jung, C.G./Jungian, 9, 11, 34-35
    on anima/animus, 15-16
    on dreams, 9-10, 25-26
    on ego, 19-20, 128
    on unconscious, 11

killing women, dream of, 92-93

ladder, dream of, 17
Leslie and Clark, 66, 70-81, 87-110
listening,, 135, 142
literal interpretation of dreams, 11
lively interactions in group therapy, 137-138, 146
Lotte and Erwin, 83-84

Mark and Debbie, 114-125
marriage 111, 112, 136
    cancelled, dream of, 121
    counseling, three stages of, 8
Martin and Hilda, 65-69, 78-79, 82
Mary and Herman, 42-45, 110-111
mass, dream of, 9-10
message of the dream, 80
monsters, dream of, 124
moons, dream of, 84, 132
mother, dream of, 84-86, 131
myths, 12

Nick and Pat, 48-52

objective and subjective interpretation of
    dreams, 10-11, 127-128
objectivity in counseling, 126
operation, dream of, 120
opinions, 138, 146
opposites, attitudinal, 35, 37
    reconciliation of, 9

parent(s), dream of, 62-63, 82
partners and dreams, 81
party, dream of, 38-40, 54, 129
passive vs. active behavior, 122-123
Pat and Nick, 48-52
penholder, dream of, 10
persona, 16-17, 40, 128
personal vs. collective unconscious, 11-12
personality, 27

pool, dream of, 89
power, 63
    dream of, 104-107
premarital counseling, 133
prognosis, 8, 44, 47-48, 130-131
project/projection, 8, 11, 17-18, 81-82,
    129, 135, 141
psychiatrists, dream of, 95-96
psychological type(s), 34-37, 129, 133,
    136
psychosis as shown in dreams, 52-53, 130
public speaking, dream of, 73-74

questions, 144-146

rapport in counseling, 134-135
reason for counseling, 48, 133-134
reconciliation of opposites, 9
relationship as client, 126
responsibility for one's opinions, 138, 146
    for dream content, 11
ringing telephone, dream of, 83-84
Rita, dream of, 88-89

same gender person in dreams, 128. *See
    also* anima; animus
scapegoating in group therapy, 139-141
Self, 23-25, 128
self in dreams, 19. *See also* ego
separated woman, dream of, 97-98
separation. *See* divorce
sexuality, 8, 91, 93-94, 103, 105
shadow, 11, 17-19, 39, 80, 128-129, 131,
    133, 135
shared vs. single life, 102
sinister character, dream of, 18-19
statement, 146. *See also* question
status symbols, 17, 40. *See also* success
structure of dreams, 26, 127
subjective and objective interpretation of
    dreams, 10-11, 127-128
subway, dream of, 61

success, 25. *See also* status symbols
superior, dream of, 125

taking sides in counseling, 100-101, 103-
   104, 113, 135
talking to, not about, 138-139
terminology in therapy, 127
therapist/therapy, 9, 11, 16, 41, 46, 55-57,
   101
   contract in, 141-142
   empathy with last speaker, 7-8
   final phase, 83-113, 131-132, 136-137
   group, 39-42, 65-82, 137-142, 146
   taking sides in, 100-101, 103-104, 113,
      135
   termination of, 82. *See also* final phase
      of
   terminology in, 127
three stages of marriage counseling, 8
Tom and Elli, 66-67, 77-78, 84-87, 100,
   133
tower, dream of, 38-39, 54, 66-68, 129

transference, 8, 81, 135-137
tree disease, dream of, 49-50, 130
true and false burden, 100-101
two women, dream of, 71-72
types/typology, 34-37, 129, 133, 136

unconscious, 11, 21, 23, 26, 33-34, 126,
   130
   and behavior, 8
   collective vs. personal, 11-13
   and conscious mind, 9, 132
universal images, 12

voice, dream of 121
   dream of God's, 23-24

water, 89
weakness of ego, 22
weaving, dream of, 13
wife eating arm, dream of, 28-29, 129
wild horse, dream of, 124
will power, 20-21

Studies in Jungian Psychology
by Jungian Analysts

Quality Paperbacks

Prices and payment in $US (except in Canada, $Cdn)

1. The Secret Raven: Conflict and Transformation
Daryl Sharp (Toronto). ISBN 0-919123-00-7. 128 pp. $18

2. The Psychological Meaning of Redemption Motifs in Fairy Tales
Marie-Louise von Franz (Zürich). ISBN 0-919123-01-5. 128 pp. $18

3. On Divination and Synchronicity: The Psychology of Meaningful Chance
Marie-Louise von Franz (Zürich). ISBN 0-919123-02-3. 128 pp. $18

4. The Owl Was a Baker's Daughter: Obesity, Anorexia and the Repressed Feminine Marion Woodman (Toronto). ISBN 0-919123-03-1. 144 pp. $18

5. Alchemy: An Introduction to the Symbolism and the Psychology
Marie-Louise von Franz (Zürich). ISBN 0-919123-04-X. 288 pp. $25

6. Descent to the Goddess: A Way of Initiation for Women
Sylvia Brinton Perera (New York). ISBN 0-919123-05-8. 112 pp. $18

8. Border Crossings: Carlos Castaneda's Path of Knowledge
Donald Lee Williams (Boulder). ISBN 0-919123-07-4. 160 pp. $18

9. Narcissism and Character Transformation: The Psychology of Narcissistic Character Disorders
Nathan Schwartz-Salant (New York). ISBN 0-919123-08-2. 192 pp. $20

11. Alcoholism and Women: The Background and the Psychology
Jan Bauer (Montreal). ISBN 0-919123-10-4. 144 pp. $18

12. Addiction to Perfection: The Still Unravished Bride
Marion Woodman (Toronto). ISBN 0-919123-11-2. 208 pp. $20

13. Jungian Dream Interpretation: A Handbook of Theory and Practice
James A. Hall, M.D. (Dallas). ISBN 0-919123-12-0. 128 pp. $18

14. The Creation of Consciousness: Jung's Myth for Modern Man
Edward F. Edinger (Los Angeles). ISBN 0-919123-13-9. 128 pp. $18

15. The Analytic Encounter: Transference and Human Relationship
Mario Jacoby (Zürich). ISBN 0-919123-14-7. 128 pp. $18

17. The Illness That We Are: A Jungian Critique of Christianity
John P. Dourley (Ottawa). ISBN 0-919123-16-3. 128 pp. $18

19. Cultural Attitudes in Psychological Perspective
Joseph L. Henderson, M.D. (San Francisco). ISBN 0-919123-18-X. 128 pp. $18

21. The Pregnant Virgin: A Process of Psychological Transformation
Marion Woodman (Toronto). ISBN 0-919123-20-1. 208 pp. $20

22. Encounter with the Self: A Jungian Commentary on William Blake's *Illustrations of the Book of Job*
Edward F. Edinger (Los Angeles). ISBN 0-919123-21-X. 80 pp. $18

23. The Scapegoat Complex: Toward a Mythology of Shadow and Guilt
Sylvia Brinton Perera (New York). ISBN 0-919123-22-8. 128 pp. $18

24. The Bible and the Psyche: Individuation Symbolism in the Old Testament
Edward F. Edinger (Los Angeles). ISBN 0-919123-23-6. 176 pp. $20

26. The Jungian Experience: Analysis and Individuation
James A. Hall, M.D. (Dallas). ISBN 0-919123-25-2. 176 pp. $20

27. Phallos: Sacred Image of the Masculine
Eugene Monick (Scranton, PA). ISBN 0-919123-26-0. 144 pp. $18

28. The Christian Archetype: A Jungian Commentary on the Life of Christ
Edward F. Edinger (Los Angeles). ISBN 0-919123-27-9. 144 pp. $18

30. Touching: Body Therapy and Depth Psychology
Deldon Anne McNeely (Lynchburg, VA). ISBN 0-919123-29-5. 128 pp. $18

31. Personality Types: Jung's Model of Typology
Daryl Sharp (Toronto). ISBN 0-919123-30-9. 128 pp. $18

32. The Sacred Prostitute: Eternal Aspect of the Feminine
Nancy Qualls-Corbett (Birmingham). ISBN 0-919123-31-7. 176 pp. $20

33. When the Spirits Come Back
Janet O. Dallett (Seal Harbor, WA). ISBN 0-919123-32-5. 160 pp. $18

34. The Mother: Archetypal Image in Fairy Tales
Sibylle Birkhäuser-Oeri (Zürich). ISBN 0-919123-33-3. 176 pp. $20

35. The Survival Papers: Anatomy of a Midlife Crisis
Daryl Sharp (Toronto). ISBN 0-919123-34-1. 160 pp. $18

37. Dear Gladys: The Survival Papers, Book 2
Daryl Sharp (Toronto). ISBN 0-919123-36-8. 144 pp. $18

39. Acrobats of the Gods: Dance and Transformation
Joan Dexter Blackmer (Wilmot Flat, NH). ISBN 0-919123-38-4. 128 pp. $18

40. Eros and Pathos: Shades of Love and Suffering
Aldo Carotenuto (Rome). ISBN 0-919123-39-2. 160 pp. $18

41. The Ravaged Bridegroom: Masculinity in Women
Marion Woodman (Toronto). ISBN 0-919123-42-2. 224 pp. $22

43. Goethe's *Faust:* Notes for a Jungian Commentary
Edward F. Edinger (Los Angeles). ISBN 0-919123-44-9. 112 pp. $18

44. The Dream Story
Donald Broadribb (Baker's Hill, Australia). ISBN 0-919123-45-7. 256 pp. $24

45. The Rainbow Serpent: Bridge to Consciousness
Robert L. Gardner (Toronto). ISBN 0-919123-46-5. 128 pp. $18

46. Circle of Care: Clinical Issues in Jungian Therapy
Warren Steinberg (New York). ISBN 0-919123-47-3. 160 pp. $18

47. Jung Lexicon: A Primer of Terms & Concepts
Daryl Sharp (Toronto). ISBN 0-919123-48-1. 160 pp. $18

48. Body and Soul: The Other Side of Illness
Albert Kreinheder (Los Angeles). ISBN 0-919123-49-X. 112 pp. $18

49. Animus Aeternus: Exploring the Inner Masculine
Deldon Anne McNeely (Lynchburg, VA). ISBN 0-919123-50-3. 192 pp. $20

50. Castration and Male Rage: The Phallic Wound
Eugene Monick (Scranton, PA). ISBN 0-919123-51-1. 144 pp. $18

51. Saturday's Child: Encounters with the Dark Gods
Janet O. Dallett (Seal Harbor, WA). ISBN 0-919123-52-X. 128 pp. $16

52. The Secret Lore of Gardening: Patterns of Male Intimacy
Graham Jackson (Toronto). ISBN 0-919123-53-8. 160 pp. $16

53. The Refiner's Fire: Memoirs of a German Girlhood
Sigrid R. McPherson (Los Angeles). ISBN 0-919123-54-6. 208 pp. $18

54. Transformation of the God-Image: Jung's *Answer to Job*
Edward F. Edinger (Los Angeles). ISBN 0-919123-55-4. 144 pp. $18

55. Getting to Know You: The Inside Out of Relationship
Daryl Sharp (Toronto). ISBN 0-919123-56-2. 128 pp. $18

56. A Strategy for a Loss of Faith: Jung's Proposal
John P. Dourley (Ottawa). ISBN 0-919123-57-0. 144 pp. $18

58. Conscious Femininity: Interviews with Marion Woodman
Introduction by Marion Woodman (Toronto). ISBN 0-919123-59-7. 160 pp. $18

59. The Middle Passage: From Misery to Meaning in Midlife
James Hollis (Houston). ISBN 0-919123-60-0. 128 pp. $18

60. The Living Room Mysteries: Patterns of Male Intimacy, Book 2
Graham Jackson (Toronto). ISBN 0-919123-61-9. 144 pp. $18

61. Chicken Little: The Inside Story *(A Jungian Romance)*
Daryl Sharp (Toronto). ISBN 0-919123-62-7. 128 pp. $18

62. Coming To Age: The Croning Years and Late-Life Transformation
Jane R. Prétat (Providence, RI). ISBN 0-919123-63-5. 144 pp. $18

63. Under Saturn's Shadow: The Wounding and Healing of Men
James Hollis (Houston). ISBN 0-919123-64-3. 144 pp. $18

65. The Mystery of the Coniunctio: Alchemical Image of Individuation
Edward F. Edinger (Los Angeles). ISBN 0-919123-67-8. 112 pp. $18

66. The Mysterium Lectures: Journey through Jung's *Mysterium Coniunctionis*
Edward F. Edinger (Los Angeles). ISBN 0-919123-66-X. 352 pp. $30

83. The Cat: A Tale of Feminine Redemption
Marie-Louise von Franz (Zurich). ISBN 0-919123-84-8. 128 pp. $18

87. The Problem of the Puer Aeternus
Marie-Louise von Franz (Zurich). ISBN 0-919123-88-0. 288 pp. $25

95. Digesting Jung: Food for the Journey
Daryl Sharp (Toronto). ISBN 0-919123-96-1. 128 pp. $18

99. The Secret World of Drawings: Healing through Art
Gregg M. Furth (New York). ISBN 1-894574-00-1. 100 illustrations. 176 pp. $25

100. Animus and Anima in Fairy Tales
Marie-Louise von Franz (Zurich). ISBN 1-894574-01-X. 128 pp. $18

108. The Sacred Psyche: A Psychological Approach to the Psalms
Edward F. Edinger (Los Angeles). ISBN 1-894574-09-5. 160 pp. $18

111. The Secret Garden: Temenos for Individuation
Margaret Eileen Meredith (Toronto). ISBN 1-894574-12-5. 160 pp. $18

112. Not the Big Sleep: on having fun, seriously *(A Jungian Romance)*
Daryl Sharp (Toronto). ISBN 1-894574-13-3. 128 pp. $18

113. The Use of Dreams in Couple Counseling
Renée Nell (Litchfield, CT). ISBN 1-894574-14-1. 160 pp. $18

Discounts: any 3-5 books, 10%; 6-9 books, 20%; 10 or more, 25%

Add Postage/Handling: 1-2 books, $6 surface ($10 air); 3-4 books, $8 surface ($12 air);

5-9 books, $15 surface ($20 air); 10 or more, $10 surface ($25 air)

Free Catalogue of **over 100 titles** and **Jung at Heart** newsletter

INNER CITY BOOKS, Box 1271, Station Q, Toronto, ON M4T 2P4, Canada
Tel. 416- 927-0355 / Fax 416-924-1814 / E-mail: sales@innercitybooks.net